Microsoft Office 365. Definitive Edition

From Basics to Advanced Tips. Discover Innovative Features with This Ultimate Guide | Practical Advice to Enhance Your Work and Life with AI.

Peter Patton

Copyright 2024 – Peter Patton © All rights reserved.

The content contained within this book may not be reproduced, duplicated, or transmitted without direct written permission from the author or the publisher.

Under no circumstances will any blame or legal responsibility be held against the publisher, or author, for any damages, reparation, or monetary loss due to the information contained within this book. Either directly or indirectly.

Legal Notice:

This book is copyright protected. This book is only for personal use. You cannot amend, distribute, sell, use, quote or paraphrase any part, or the content within this book, without the consent of the author or publisher.

Disclaimer Notice:

Please note the information contained within this document is for educational and entertainment purposes only. All effort has been executed to present accurate, up to date, and reliable, complete information. No warranties of any kind are declared or implied. Readers acknowledge that the author is not engaging in the rendering of legal, financial, medical, or professional advice. The content within this book has been derived from various sources. Please consult a licensed professional before attempting any techniques outlined in this book.

By reading this document, the reader agrees that under no circumstances is the author responsible for any losses, direct or indirect, which are incurred because of the use of information contained within this document, including, but not limited to, errors, omissions, or inaccuracies.

Table of contents

INTRODUCTION 12

1. GET STARTED WITH OFFICE 365 13

   1.1 AVAILABLE VERSIONS AND PLANS 13

   1.2 SYSTEM REQUIREMENTS 13

   1.3 INSTALLATION AND ACTIVATION 14

2. OFFICE 365 ACCOUNT MANAGEMENT 15

   2.1 MANAGING ACCOUNT SETTINGS 15

   2.2 SECURITY AND PRIVACY MANAGEMENT 15

   2.3 PASSWORD RECOVERY AND RESET 16

3. MICROSOFT WORD 2025 17

   THE NEW FEATURES OF MICROSOFT WORD 2025 17

      How to get Microsoft Word 2025 18

   MAIN FUNCTIONS 18

      Automation and time savings... 19

   HOME... 19

      Notes 20

      Font 20

      Paragraph.. 21

      Styles 22

      5.   Modification 23

      Dictation 24

   INSERT.. 24

      1. Pages 25

      Tables 25

      Illustrations 25

      Add-ons 26

      Links 26

      Text... 27

      Symbols 27

   DRAW... 28

      1. Pens 28

      Ink to Text.. 29

      Tires 29

      Additional Tools 30

      Freehand drawing 30

   LAYOUT... 31

      Page Setup 31

      Paragraph.. 32

      Arrange 32

   REFERENCES... 33

Table of Contents...33

Footnotes...34

Citations and bibliography...35

Captions 36

Cross-references..36

MAILINGS 37

Create..37

Start Mail Merge..38

Select recipients..38

Insert merge fields 39

Preview Results 39

Finalize and merge..39

REVIEW..39

Spelling and grammar check 40

Research..40

Language...40

Remarks...41

Track Changes..41

Protection 42

VIEW..42

Document views 43

Zoom 43

Window..43

Macros 44

HELP..44

Search 45

Support 45

Feedback 45

Syntax and Fluency...46

Customizing Suggestions 46

ADVANCED TIPS 46

Advanced Find and Replace 47

Creating Custom Styles..47

4. MICROSOFT EXCEL 2025 49

INTRODUCTION TO EXCEL 2025 49

Why learn Excel? Benefits and practical applications..49

Key Features and Uses..49

HOME...50

Clipboard 50

Character...51

Alignment..51

Number..51

Styles 51

Cells 52

EDIT 52

INSERT 53

    Calculator 53

    Graphs 54

    Illustrations 55

    Add-ons 55

    Sparkline Chart Thumbnails 55

    Filters 55

    Links 56

    Symbols 56

DRAW 56

PAGE LAYOUT 57

FORMULAS 58

    Function Library 58

    Define names 59

    Formula Checker 60

    Calculation 60

DATE 61

    Get & Transform Data 61

    Range and connections 62

    Sorting and filtering 62

    Data Tools 63

    Forecasts 63

    Data Analysis 64

REVIEW 64

    Spell check 65

    Accessibility 65

    Translation 65

    Remarks 65

    Notes 65

    Protection 66

    Track Changes 66

VIEW 67

    Workbook Views 67

    Show 67

    Zoom 68

    Window 68

    Macros 68

5. MICROSOFT POWERPOINT 2025 70

ESSENTIAL FEATURES FOR PRESENTATIONS 70

HOW TO GET AND USE POWERPOINT FOR FREE 70

HOME 71

    Paste 71

    Slides 72

Text formatting 72

Inserting Images and Shapes 73

Share with OneDrive 73

Remarks 73

Record 74

Enter 74

Slides 74

Tables 75

Images 75

Shapes 75

Icons 76

3D Models 76

Charts 76

Links 76

Text boxes 77

WordArt 77

Slide Numbers 77

Equations and Symbols 77

Video 78

Audio 78

Drawing 78

Design 79

Eraser 79

Lasso selection 79

Pen Types 79

Ink to Text 79

Inserting Shapes and Equations 80

Design 80

Themes 80

Variants 80

Background 81

Designer 81

Graphic effects 81

Transitions 82

Preview Transitions 82

Selecting transitions 82

Effect Options 83

Duration 83

Audio 83

Slide Progress 83

Animations 84

Types of animations 84

Effect Options 85

Animation Pane 85

Advanced Animation 85

Preview 86

Duration 86

Customizing and enhancing animations 86

SLIDE SHOW 87

Start Slide Show 87

Presenter View 88

Set Up Presentation 88

Hide Slide 88

Intervals 88

Audio narration and intervals 88

Audio 89

Subtitles 89

Monitor 89

RECORDS 89

Record Presentation 90

Export your slideshow as a video 90

Personalization of the recording 90

Audio and Video Options 91

Playback of the recording 91

Re-Register 91

REVISION 92

Spell check 92

Translation 93

Remarks 93

Intelligent Search (Search Insights) 93

Language 93

Accessibility 93

Paragraphs and text direction 94

SHOW 94

How to view the presentation 94

Schematics 95

Precision Instruments 96

Zoom 96

Macros 97

OTHER 97

Graphic formatting 97

Arrangement and layering 98

Size and Aspect Ratio 98

Text Box 98

Specific formats 99

Applying transitions to slides 99

Creating animations for text and objects 100

When and how to use animations and transitions 100

ADVANCED TIPS 101

Techniques to make presentations more effective 101

Using PowerPoint's advanced features *101*

Time and Evidence Management *102*

Securing and sharing presentations *102*

6. MICROSOFT OUTLOOK 2025 .... **103**

CRITICAL FEATURES OF OUTLOOK 2025 103

A platform for modern work *104*

ADVANCED EMAIL MANAGEMENT 104

Focused Inbox *104*

Snooze emails *105*

3. Filters and rules for automation *105*

Labels and categories *105*

Quick Storage *105*

SYNCHRONIZATION WITH OTHER OFFICE APPLICATIONS 106

Built-in calendars *106*

Scheduling meetings *106*

Microsoft Teams integration *107*

Automatic scheduling suggestions *107*

Sync with other calendars *107*

TIPS AND SHORTCUTS 108

Automations with rules and filters *108*

Using Smart Folders *108*

Automation with Power Automate *108*

Custom folders and categories *109*

Quick Responses and Actions *109*

ADDING MULTIPLE ACCOUNTS 110

How to add a new email account on Outlook *110*

Benefits of having multiple accounts integrated into Outlook *111*

7. MICROSOFT TEAMS 2025 .... **112**

WHY USE MICROSOFT TEAMS 2025? 112

Microsoft Teams for modern work *113*

HOW TO SET UP AND ORGANIZE A TEAM 113

Create a new team *114*

Organize channels *114*

Configure access and security settings *114*

Invite external guests *115*

Task Management and Tracking *115*

SCHEDULING AND MANAGING VIRTUAL MEETINGS 115

Scheduling a virtual meeting *116*

CONDUCTING A VIRTUAL MEETING 116

Meeting Recording and Reporting *116*

Outlook Integration for Scheduling *117*

Hybrid Meetings and Teams Rooms *117*

Real-time conversations *117*

FILE SHARING AND MANAGEMENT 118
    Research and organize conversations 118
    Security settings and permissions on files 119
    Establish clear communication channels 119
    Schedule regular meetings 119
    Collaborate on documents in real-time 120
    Time and task management 120
    A synchronization of communications 120

8.   MICROSOFT ONENOTE 2025 121

GET STARTED WITH ONENOTE 121
WHAT MAKES ONENOTE UNIQUE? 122
    An intuitive and integrated work environment 122
    An application for every context 122
    Advanced clipboard management 123
    Sections: Organizing Information into Chapters 123
    Pages and subpages: Detailing information 123
    Labels and categories: Organize and retrieve information quickly 124
    Using Templates for a Consistent Structure 124
HOW TO SHARE AND COLLABORATE ON NOTES AND PROJECTS 124
    Sharing notebooks 125
    Real-time collaboration 125
    Permit and security management 125
    Version History 126
    Integration with other applications for smoother collaboration 126
ADVANCED CLIPBOARD MANAGEMENT 126
    1. Sync between devices 127
    Efficient use of sections 127
    Managing pages and subpages 127
    Quick Notes and Audio Recordings 128
    Integration with Power Automate for automation 128
INTEGRATION WITH OUTLOOK AND OTHER APPLICATIONS 129
    Outlook Integration: Notes and Meetings 129
    Microsoft Teams Integration: Collaboration and Sharing 130
    SharePoint Integration: Document Storage and Management 130
    Automation and integration with Power Automate 131
ADVANCED TIPS 131
    Using Page Templates to Standardize Notes 131
    Visual organization with the use of labels and colors 131
    Create hyperlinks between pages 132
    Take advantage of OneNote's advanced search 132
    Use OneNote for project management 132
    Automate repetitive tasks with Power Automate 133

9.   MICROSOFT ACCESS 2025 134

INTRODUCTION TO MICROSOFT ACCESS... 134
    A user-friendly interface and powerful tools... 135
    Relational Data Management 135
    Create custom applications 135
    Integration with other Microsoft applications 135
CREATING AND MANAGING DATABASES 136
    Creating a new database.. 136
    Table management 136
    Data Normalization 137
    Relationships between tables.. 137
    Data maintenance and updating... 138
DATA ANALYSIS WITH ADVANCED QUERIES... 138
    Select Query.. 139
    Parametric queries 139
    Append and Update Queries.. 139
    Table Creation Query 140
    Merge queries and cross-queries 140
    Query optimization.. 140
ADVANCED DATABASE CONSTRUCTION 141
    Creating Relational Tables... 141
    Setting up table relationships 142
    Referential integrity and validation rules.. 142
    Performance Optimization with the Use of Indexes 142
    Transaction Management and Rollback 143
    Database Backup and Restore... 143
PROCESS AUTOMATION WITH MACROS 143
    What are macros in Microsoft Access?... 143
    Creating a Macro in Access 144
    Types of Macros in Access... 144
    Automate workflows with macros 144
    Macro integration with other Microsoft applications... 145
    Use of advanced macros and interaction with VBA 145
DATA BACKUP AND PROTECTION 145
    Importance of Regular Backup.. 146
    How to make a backup in Access.. 146
    Database Restore 146
    Password protection of the database.. 147
    Saving the database to the cloud 147

10.   MICROSOFT ONEDRIVE 2025 .... **149**

GET STARTED WITH ONEDRIVE.. 149
    Sync and share files securely... 149
FILE ORGANIZATION FOR COLLABORATIVE PROJECTS 150
    File management tips... 150
    Automation of backup and synchronization processes 150

Automatic Backup 151

File Recovery 151

Selective Sync 151

Microsoft 365 integration.. 151

11. MICROSOFT 365 COPILOT.. 153

KEY FEATURES 153

Automated Content Creation... 154

Email management.. 154

Meeting Support 154

Data Analysis and Visualization 154

Integration with Microsoft 365 Chat.. 154

12. ADVANCED TIPS AND TRICKS 156

AUTOMATE REPETITIVE TASKS WITH POWER AUTOMATE 156

What is Power Automate, and how does it work? 156

Examples of common workflows 157

Benefits of using Power Automate... 157

FAQ 158

CONCLUSION 162

Introduction

Welcome to the Office 365 hands-on manual! If you're about to start your journey with Office 365 and are looking for a simple and straightforward way to figure out how to best use it, you've come to the right place. This manual is created especially for you, who want to learn how to use these tools without complications and with minimal effort.

Let's start with the basics: Office 365 is a productivity suite from Microsoft that gives you a range of applications and services designed to make your work and daily life easier. Whether you're looking to draft documents, make presentations, collaborate with others, or manage your files, Office 365 has something useful for you. Each application is designed to help you get things done faster and more organized. Throughout this manual, I'll walk you through every single Office 365 tool and service. We'll start with setting up your account, showing you how to set it up and customize it to fit your needs. I'll walk you through how to make the most of Word, Excel, PowerPoint, and Outlook, with practical examples that will help you understand how to use these applications in your daily work. We'll look at how to use Word to create professional documents, how Excel will help you manage and analyze data with ease, and how PowerPoint can make your presentations truly memorable. In addition, you will learn how to use Outlook to organize your emails and manage your calendar effortlessly.

Each section of the manual is designed to be clear and practical, with step-by-step explanations and helpful tips to put what you've learned into practice right away. Don't worry if it seems like a lot to learn at first: with our straightforward and hands-on approach, you'll be able to master each tool without any problems.

By the end of this manual, you'll not only know how to use Office 365, but you'll also have the skills you need to manage your work more efficiently and productively. You'll learn how to set up and customize your work environment, how to use core applications, and how to collaborate with others effectively. Simply put, you'll be ready to unlock the full potential of Office 365 and work like a pro.

To help you further enhance your skills and better manage your time between work and family, I've prepared **6 exclusive bonuses** for you that utilize various apps from the Office 365 suite. These bonuses are specifically designed for professionals like you who are eager to boost productivity, discover advanced features, and feel more confident tackling new work challenges. To learn more and start leveraging these resources right away, please go to peterpatton365.com or scan the QR code with your phone.

I am happy to have the opportunity to guide you on this path. Grab the manual and let's get started together to discover all that Office 365 has to offer. We're here to help you take a big leap toward simpler, more productive work management. Let's start!

1. Get started with Office 365

Let's start with a simple question: what exactly is Office 365? You may already have an idea, but let's try to shed some light. Office 365 is a cloud-based productivity suite developed by Microsoft. In simple words, it is a set of applications and services that you can use both online and offline to manage practically every aspect of your daily work. It includes tools you're probably already familiar with, such as Word, Excel, PowerPoint, and Outlook, as well as more specific applications like Teams for collaboration, OneDrive for cloud storage, and SharePoint for document and project management.

What makes Office 365 so powerful is its ability to sync everything you do between different devices: computers, tablets, smartphones. This means you can start working on a document in the office, continue at home from your laptop, and maybe do a final touch-up on your phone while you're on the go. Everything is always up to date and at your fingertips. Plus, Office 365 is constantly being updated with new features and improvements from Microsoft, so you don't have to worry about falling behind with the latest tech news.

1.1 Available Versions and Plans

Now that you know what Office 365 is, let's see together the different versions and plans that Microsoft offers. You may think that Office 365 is a single package, but there are several options to choose from, each designed to meet specific needs. Microsoft offers plans for personal use, for small and medium-sized businesses, and for large enterprises.

If you need Office 365 for personal or family use, there's Office 365 Personal, which is meant for a single user, and Office 365 Family, which you can share with up to six people. Both offer full access to all the main applications and a good amount of OneDrive storage.

For small and medium-sized businesses, there are plans like Microsoft 365 Business Basic, Standard, and Premium. Each plan offers a mix of applications and services, with differences that mainly relate to access to advanced security tools and IT management capacity. On the other hand, if you're looking for something for a large enterprise, Microsoft 365 Enterprise plans include more advanced security, compliance, and IT management features.

Each of these plans is available as a monthly or annual subscription; So, you can choose the option that best suits your needs and budget. In any case, all plans include continuous updates, so you will always have access to the latest versions of applications and new features.

1.2 System Requirements

Before you start with your Office 365 installation, it's important to make sure that your device meets the system requirements. Don't worry, you don't need to have a supercomputer to run Office 365, but it's still helpful to know what it takes to ensure a smooth experience.

For Windows, Office 365 requires at least Windows 10. If you're using a Mac, you should have macOS 10.14 (Mojave) or later. As for hardware, you'll need at least 4GB of RAM (although 8GB is preferable for more fluidity) and 4GB of available hard drive space. An internet connection is also critical, not only for the initial installation but also for using cloud features and keeping applications up to date.

If you want to use Office 365 on a mobile device, such as an iPad or Android phone, make sure your operating system is up to date: iOS requires at least version 13, while Android requires version 6.0 or later. Also make sure you have enough free space for installing apps.

1.3 Installation and Activation

Once you've verified that your device meets the requirements, you're ready to proceed with installing and activating Office 365. Don't worry, it's a pretty simple process, and I'll walk you through each step.

To get started, go to the official Office 365 website and sign in to your Microsoft account. If you don't have an account yet, you'll be prompted to create one. After logging in, go to the download section and download the installation file. Once the download is complete, open the file and follow the on-screen instructions. During installation, you will be asked to choose the location where you want to install applications. If you're not sure, you can simply leave the default settings.

Once the installation is complete, launch one of the Office applications, such as Word or Excel. You will be asked to activate the product. Here, you will need to enter your Microsoft account and follow the instructions to complete the activation. Once activated, Office 365 is ready to use. You can start exploring all the applications and features you have available.

Remember that with your subscription you have access to all the main applications, continuous updates and a series of cloud services that will allow you to work from anywhere. With these foundations, you're ready to immerse yourself in the world of Office 365 and make the most of its potential. Moving on!

2. Office 365 Account Management

To get started with Office 365, you first need to create and set up your account. This step is essential because it allows you to access all the applications and services included in your subscription.

To begin with, go to Microsoft's official website and click on "Create an account" if you don't already have one. You will be asked to enter an email address you will use as your username. You can use an existing address or create a new one directly with Microsoft. Once you've entered your email, you must choose a secure password. Remember to use uppercase and lowercase letters, numbers, and symbols to make your password more secure.

After creating the account, the next step is to set it up. When you first log in, you'll be asked to verify your email address and complete some basic information, such as your name, date of birth, and country. This helps personalize your Office 365 experience and ensure your account is secure.

Once you've set it up, you'll be ready to start using Office 365. You will access your dashboard to find all the applications and services available. From here, you'll be able to manage your settings, access your documents, and explore all that Office 365 offers.

2.1 Managing Account Settings

Once you've created your account, you must know how to manage your settings to customize the experience to suit your needs. Microsoft gives you plenty of options for doing this and knowing where to go and what to do can improve your use of Office 365.

From your account dashboard, you can access your settings by clicking on your profile photo (or the user icon if you still need to upload an image) in the top right. Here, you'll find several options that allow you to edit your profile information, such as your name and picture, and manage your contact preferences. If you prefer to receive email notifications or want to change your language and time zone settings, this is the place to do it.

One of the most valuable options is managing your subscriptions. Here, you can see which services and applications are included in your plan, check the status of your subscription, and renew or change your plan if necessary. You can also manage your OneDrive storage, checking how much space you've used and purchasing additional space if needed.

2.2 Security and Privacy Management

Security and privacy are paramount when it comes to your Office 365 account. Microsoft takes these matters very seriously, but you also have an essential role in protecting your account. Let's look at what you can do to keep your account secure.

First, I recommend enabling two-factor authentication (2FA). This is an additional step that requires, in addition to the password, a code that is sent to you over the phone or through an authenticator app. That way, even if someone discovers your password, they still can't access your account without the code. You can enable 2FA from your account's security settings. Additionally, it would help if you regularly looked at your account's recent activity section. Here, you can see if there have been suspicious or unrecognized logins to your account and, if necessary, take steps such as changing your password or disconnecting suspicious devices.

Regarding privacy, Office 365 provides several tools that allow you to fine-tune who can access your information and how it's used. Microsoft treats your personal data carefully, complying with data protection regulations such as the GDPR. You can access your privacy settings to see exactly what data Microsoft collects, such as your name, email address, usage preferences, and activity history. You have complete control over this data: You can limit the collection of certain information or prevent it from being used for specific purposes, such as improving services or personalizing experiences. This allows you to have complete control over how your data is handled, ensuring that it is protected and only used in the way you want.

2.3 Password Recovery and Reset

Forgetting your account password can happen to anyone. Still, there's no need to worry – recovering or resetting your Office 365 password is quick and easy. If you can't access your account, go to the Office 365 login page and click "Forgot Password." At this point, you'll be asked to enter the email address or phone number associated with your account. Microsoft will send you a verification code via email or text message. Enter the code in the field indicated, and you can choose a new password. Remember to choose one that is safe, using a combination of letters, numbers, and symbols, and that you haven't used before.

If you've turned on two-factor authentication, you must confirm your identity with a second method, such as an authenticator app or an SMS code, before you can reset your password. Once you've completed this step, you'll be ready to log back into your account and resume your activities.

Here's a practical tip to simplify your life: use a password-saving tool built into the Chrome browser, Edge, or Apple's Keychain. These tools securely store your passwords and allow you to quickly log in to your account without typing them in every time. Not only do they make logging in faster and more convenient, but they also offer a higher level of security than older methods, such as spreadsheets or, even worse, password notebooks. The latter are now a bygone era and do not guarantee adequate information protection.

If you need help resetting your password or completing the process, remember to contact Microsoft Support for assistance. They help you solve any difficulties and get you back up and running quickly.

By following these tips, you can manage your password quickly and securely, ensuring quick and secure access to your Office 365 account. With this critical aspect under control, you're ready to make the most of all the features Office 365 offers. Let's move forward together on this path!

3. Microsoft Word 2025

Microsoft Word has been one of the most popular writing tools for decades, used by millions of people around the world. With its wide range of features, it allows you to create and edit documents in a simple and intuitive way, offering solutions both for writing simple texts and for managing more complex projects such as reports, technical documents, and company presentations.

Microsoft Word's importance lies in its ability to simplify the writing and formatting process. Thanks to a user-friendly interface and advanced tools that save time, it improves efficiency and quality of work. With the 2025 version, new features are introduced that make the program even more versatile and powerful, improving the user experience and offering more opportunities for customization and automation.

Introduction to Microsoft Word 2025

Microsoft Word has long been the reference point for those who need a versatile and powerful program for creating and managing documents. It's a critical tool for writing, editing, and sharing information, whether making a simple text document or a more complex project, such as a business report or a college thesis.

Why is Microsoft Word crucial?

Microsoft Word's universal diffusion and compatibility with a wide range of formats make it the ideal tool for those who work in business, education, research, or simply for those who need to manage everyday documents. It is a writing tool and a complete work environment capable of offering advanced formatting features, managing images, charts, tables, text reviews, and real-time collaboration.

In the professional context, Word has become essential not only for creating documents but also for **collaborating with** colleagues, clients, and partners. The ability to easily share files, work on a document simultaneously, and use review tools can speed up decision-making and improve efficiency. Similarly, in the personal sphere, it is an ideal tool for creative projects, from writing personal letters to creating visually appealing documents.

The new features of Microsoft Word 2025

Version 2025 introduces several updates and **improved features** that make Word even more intuitive and productive. These enhancements are designed to meet the needs of modern professionals who need to manage multiple tasks, collaborate with teams, and work faster and more efficiently.

Here are some of the main new features introduced in this release:

1. **Improved collaboration**: One of the key features of the new version of Word is the increased integration with Office 365 collaboration tools. Now, it's even easier to share documents in real-time, with the ability to track changes made by colleagues and provide immediate feedback through feedback. This feature is handy for those working remotely or in teams spread across multiple locations.
2. **Advanced automation**: Word 2025 includes new automation options, such as creating **custom macros** to speed up repetitive tasks. These features save time and reduce the margin for human error by allowing you to quickly apply standard layouts and formatting.
3. **Optimized user interface**: Microsoft has refined the user interface to make it even more intuitive, with **customizable tabs** and a toolbar that adapts to your needs. This means that, depending on

your work, Word will show you the most relevant options, reducing the need to navigate through numerous menus.

4. **New formatting options**: Text and image formatting management has been improved to make it easier to create aesthetically pleasing documents. The 2025 version introduces a broader range of themes, styles, and layout options, allowing you to customize your documents without needing external software.

5. **Deeper integration with the cloud**: With deeper integration with **OneDrive** and **SharePoint**, Word 2025 allows you to automatically save documents to the cloud, ensuring your work is always protected and accessible from any device. Not only does this improve data security, but it also facilitates multi-device collaboration.

6. **Brilliant Review**: With Word 2025, automated review features have been enhanced through artificial intelligence, which suggests improvements to the text in terms of grammar, spelling, style, **and tone**. This tool is handy for those who need to write formal documents or content intended for publication.

How to get Microsoft Word 2025

To make the most of all these new features, you can get Word 2025 through several options. Microsoft offers Word as an integral part of the **Microsoft Office 365 package**, including other valuable applications such as Excel, PowerPoint, and Teams. This allows for seamless integration between the various instruments, optimizing productivity. In addition, Word can be purchased as a standalone application or used as a free web version, albeit with limited functionality.

Main functions

Microsoft Word has become one of the most comprehensive and flexible word-processing tools available. It's so prevalent not only because of its ability to create textual documents but also because of the wide range of **advanced features** that simplify and improve the entire process of drafting, editing, and collaborating. Learning to use Word thoroughly can transform your productivity, allowing you to complete projects more efficiently and with a higher level of professionalism.

One of the main reasons why Word is so widely adopted is its **simple and intuitive interface**. Even for beginners, the logical structure of commands and menus allows you to start writing and formatting documents in minutes. Everything is easily accessible through the ribbon (or "Ribbon"), divided into tabs that group the tools into logical categories: insertion, layout, references, review, etc. This interface makes learning more accessible and reduces the time to perform complex tasks, such as managing tables or creating automatic indexes.

One of the significant advantages of Word is its wide range of **formatting options**. You can customize every aspect of your document, from margins to text size, colors to fonts, and the arrangement of images and tables. Word provides a set of **predefined styles** that you can easily apply to ensure consistency throughout your document. These styles help maintain consistent formatting for headings, subheadings, paragraphs, and captions. If you want a more personalized look, you can edit or create new styles, ensuring each document meets your needs.

For those who need to work with **long and complex documents**, such as business reports, theses, or reports, Word offers tools to simplify the management of this content. Automatic **tables of content**, cross-references, **footnotes,** and **headers help** you organize your information in a clear and accessible way. In addition, Word allows you to divide your document into **sections** with different formatting, efficiently managing page breaks, orientation, and custom headers for each part of the document. This level of control is essential for those working on complex or multi-section projects, which require a structured and professional presentation. In addition to text, Word allows you to easily insert **images, charts, tables, SmartArt**, and other visual elements, improving your documents' understanding and attractiveness. With the "Drag and Drop" feature, you can place your images exactly where you want them. The **image formatting** tools allow you to change their size, position, and alignment with text quickly and easily. In addition, Word supports a wide range of graphic formats and will enable you to integrate dynamic content, such as Excel tables and charts, which update automatically when edited in the source file. This is especially useful for business reports or presentations that must be updated regularly.

In the modern world of work, **collaboration is** critical. Microsoft Word excels in this area, offering tools that facilitate **review and teamwork**. With the **comment** function and **review** mode, multiple users can work on the same document, making changes and adding feedback without altering the integrity of the original text. Track **Changes** mode lets you see who made what change, making it easier to manage feedback and finalize the document. Combined with OneDrive or SharePoint, you can work in real-time with others, making the collaboration process faster and less error prone.

Automation and time savings

Word also offers advanced **automation** features to simplify repetitive tasks and increase efficiency. These include creating custom **macros that** automate actions such as formatting paragraphs or inserting recurring elements (e.g., signatures, company logos, text templates). This automation capability is handy for those who work with large documents or those who frequently need to create the same document type with slight variations. Using macros means reducing the time spent on manual operations, avoiding errors, and improving productivity.

Another critical advantage of Word is its **compatibility** with other formats, including PDF, ODT (OpenDocument), and plain text formats. You can easily export your documents to PDF format for secure and professional distribution or import them into other formats without losing formatting. In addition, Word offers several options for sharing documents: email files directly from the application, share them via links on **OneDrive** or collaborate in real-time using **Teams or** SharePoint.

Home

The **Home** tab in Microsoft Word is the hub for all major writing and formatting tasks. Here, users can quickly access the most common tools for editing and managing text, paragraphs, and notes. This tab is designed to provide the essential basic functionality and instant access to the formatting tools you need to create a clear, readable document.

Notes

The **Clipboard** section contains the tools you need to cut, copy, and paste text or objects into your document.

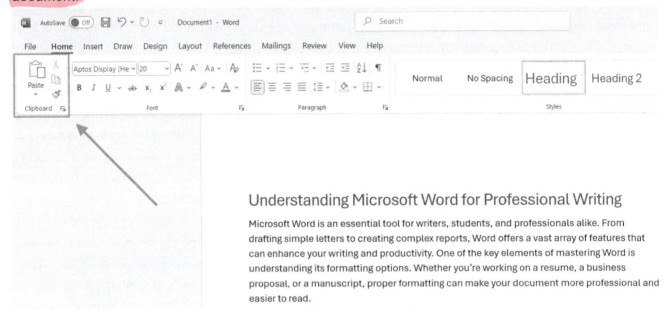

- **Cut**: (Ctrl + X) Removes the selected text or object and copies it to the clipboard, so you can paste it elsewhere.
- **Copy**: (Ctrl + C) Duplicates the selected content to the clipboard without removing it from the document.
- **Paste**: (Ctrl + V) Inserts the copied or cut content from the clipboard where the cursor is located.
- **Paste Special**: Allows you to paste while keeping the original format or pasting only the unformatted text.

Font

This section covers all the tools for formatting text, allowing you to customize the font's appearance in your document.

- **Bold**: (Ctrl + B) Makes text thicker and more marked to emphasize importance.
- **Italic**: (Ctrl + I) Skew text, often used to emphasize a word or phrase.
- **Underline**: (Ctrl + U) Adds a line below the text.
- **Strikethrough**: Draws a line through the text, indicating that it has been erased or corrected.
- **Superscript**: Raises text above the baseline, valid for mathematical exponents or notes.
- **Subscript**: Place the text below the baseline, as in the case of chemical formulas (e.g. H_2O).
- **Case**: Change the selected text to uppercase, lowercase, or other capitalization variations.
- **Font**: Change the font style from Times New Roman to Calibri.
- **Font size**: Change the text size to one that is selectable from a list or by typing a value.
- **Font Color**: Change the color of the text to highlight or stylize it.
- **Highlighter**: Simulates a highlighter, applying a background color to the selected text.

- **Text Effects**: Add effects such as shadows, reflections, glows, and more to the text for customization.

Imagine you're writing a report. For the title, you can choose a large font size, such as **Calibri** in **size 20**, and make it **bold** to stand out. You can select **Calibri** in **size 12** for the main text. Let's say you want to emphasize a crucial point; you can make it **italic** or change the **text color** to blue.

1. Select the text you want to modify.
2. Go to the Font section and choose the font type and size from the dropdown menu.
3. To apply bold, italic, or underline, click on the respective icon (B for bold, I for italic, U for underline).
4. Use the text color icon to choose a different color.

Paragraph

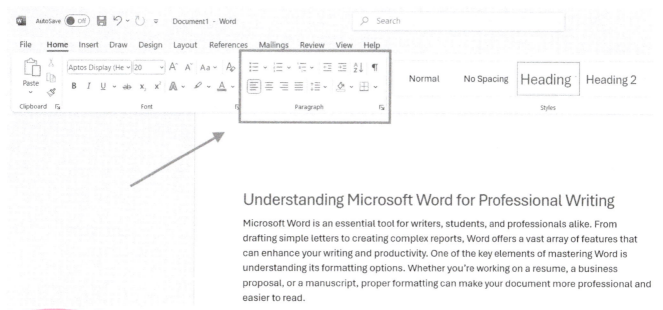

The **Paragraph** section handles the alignment and arrangement of text into blocks.
- **Alignment**: Align the text within the paragraph:
    - **Left** (Ctrl + L): Aligns the text along the left margin.
    - **Centered** (Ctrl + E): Center the text on the page.
    - **Right** (Ctrl + R): Aligns the text along the right margin.
    - **Justified** (Ctrl + J): Distributes text evenly across the margins, creating a formal and uncluttered look.
- **Line Spacing** controls the distance between lines in a paragraph. Common options include single, 1.5-line, and double spacing.
- **Paragraph Spacing**: Increases or decreases the space between paragraphs, which helps improve readability.
- **Bulleted lists**: Create a list with symbols such as bullets or icons.
- **Numbered Lists**: Generate an ordered list with numbers or letters.

- **Multi-level lists**: You can create sub-level lists for a more complex structure.
- **Increase/Decrease Indent**: Move the text to the right or left, changing the margins to create an indent.
- **Borders**: Adds borders around the paragraph or a specific selection.

Suppose you're creating a task list for a project. You can use bullet points to organize the list cleanly. If you're outlining steps for a procedure, use a numbered list for logical order. You can use justified alignment for longer paragraphs to make the text uniform on both sides.

1. Select the paragraph or text you want to format.
2. In the Paragraph section, click on Bullets or Numbering to turn the text into a list.
3. Position the text using the alignment icons (left, center, right, right, justified).
4. Click on your icons or select spacing options from the dropdown to add indents or adjust the spacing between paragraph menus.

Styles

The **Styles** section is crucial for providing consistent and professional formatting for your document. Predefined styles allow you to apply standard formatting with one click.

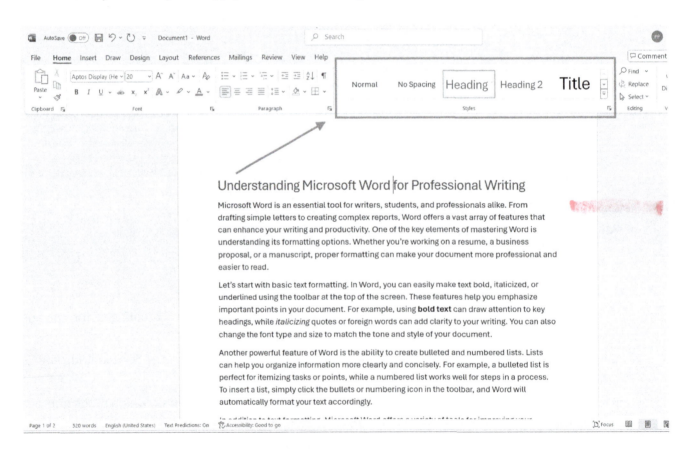

- **Normal**: Applies the default paragraph style.

- **Heading 1, Heading 2, Heading 3**: Default heading styles help structure your document and generate an automatic table of contents.
- **Citation**: Apply stylistic formatting for citations within the text.
- **Emphasis**: Format text with italics or other highlights to make it stand out.
- **Create/edit styles**: Allows you to create or customize existing styles, making the document customized and uniform in all its parts.

Imagine you're drafting a lengthy report with multiple sections. You can apply Heading 1 to main titles, 2 to subheadings, and Normal to body text. This makes the document organized and easy to navigate. At the end, you can insert a table of contents with just a click, and Word will automatically update page numbers and sections.

5. Select the text you want to turn into a heading or subheading.
6. Go to the Styles section and choose Heading 1 for a main title, Heading 2 for a subheading, and Normal for regular body text.
7. To create a table of contents, go to the References tab and search for Contents. Word will automatically generate an index based on the headings and subheadings you've applied.

If you're working on a long document with multiple levels of headings, like "Heading 1," "Heading 2," and "Heading 3," use Word's default settings for these styles. Once the draft is complete, adjust the font, size, line spacing, and paragraph spacing for each style during the final formatting phase, selecting what best fits your document. This approach will save time, as you can apply final modifications across the document in a single step. Highlight the desired Word or phrase, right-click on the heading section, and select "Update Heading to Match Selection." This way, all words or phrases with that specific style will update to the highlighted style.

5. Modification

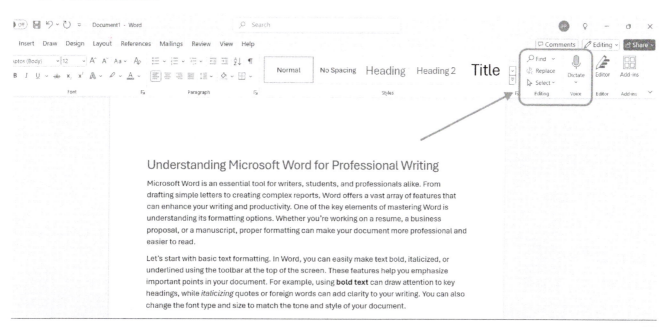

The **Edit** section provides practical tools for quickly navigating, searching, and editing text within the document.
- **Find** (Ctrl + F): Search for specific words or phrases within the document.
- **Replace** (Ctrl + H): Find and replace one word or phrase with another, saving time in long documents.
- **Select**: Select all text in the document or only specific parts, such as objects or similarly formatted text.

Dictation

Dictation is a modern addition to the **Home tab**, which allows users to enter text using their voice. It's beneficial for those who prefer voice writing or those who need to quickly transcribe thoughts or notes without typing.

Insert

The **Insert** tab in Microsoft Word allows you to enrich your document by adding various elements, such as images, charts, tables, links, and more. This tab offers tools to insert objects that improve the presentation of the document, making it more interactive, visually appealing, and structured.

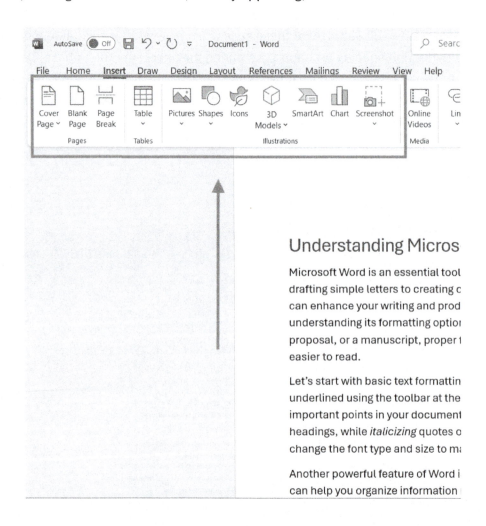

1. Pages

The **Pages section** is useful for managing the organization of the document by inserting new pages or changing their arrangement.

- **Cover page**: Adds a preformatted cover page to the document, with attractive designs and spaces to insert information such as title, author, and date.
- **Blank Page**: This option inserts a new blank page at the cursor point, which is useful for separating sections or chapters.
- **Page break** (Ctrl + Enter): Inserts a forced page break, moving the following content to a new page.

Tables

The **Tables** section provides tools for creating and customizing tables, making organizing and presenting data within the document easy.

- **Insert table**: This allows you to create a table by specifying the number of rows and columns.
- **Draw Table**: A drawing tool to create custom tables, manually plotting the rows and columns.
- **Quick Table**: Adds preformatted tables with predefined layouts, such as calendars or organized data tables.

Tables are very useful in Word, especially if you need to present data clearly and professionally. A quick note: if you're working with a standard format, like **US Letter** (8.5 x 11 inches), table insertion can easily be managed with Word's standard formatting options. However, if you're using a smaller paper size, such as 5x8 inches or 6x9 inches (commonly used for magazines or pocket-sized books), inserting tables can be more challenging, as just a few cells can take up a large portion of the page.

In 95% of cases, when using Word, we work with the classic 8.5x11 inch size or **A4** in some European countries, so this usually isn't an issue. However, it's worth noting that for smaller sizes, you may need to spend additional time on final formatting, mainly if the document contains tables (or images).

Illustrations

The **Illustrations section** allows you to insert different graphic elements, which help enrich the content and make it more visually attractive.

- **Images**: Insert images from your computer or online sources.
- **Online images**: You can search for and insert images directly from sources on the web, such as Bing or OneDrive.
- **Shapes**: This option adds predefined shapes (lines, rectangles, arrows, etc.) that can be used to create custom diagrams or illustrations.
- **SmartArt**: Inserts SmartArt charts to visually represent processes, hierarchies, cycles, relationships, etc.
- **Graphs**: Create and insert graphs (e.g., bar, pie, line) to display data clearly and concisely.
- **Screenshot**: Capture screenshots from your computer and insert them into your document.

Add-ons

The **Add-ins section** allows you to extend Word's functionality by using additional tools available in the Microsoft Store.

- **Add-ins**: Opens the Microsoft Store, where you can install third-party tools that improve efficiency and add special features.

Add-ons were prevalent a few years ago, with third-party applications integrating seamlessly into Word. Examples include instant translators, advanced syntax checkers like **Grammarly**, external dictionaries, or text-to-speech readers. Today, these add-ons still exist some are lightweight and quite useful (depending on your profession), while others have become obsolete. Many of these extra features have been integrated and improved directly in Word over time. This is the strength of the **Office 365 suite**: it offers versatility and scalability across the various applications included in the package. With this continuous evolution, it's likely that, in the not-too-distant future, add-ons might even become a thing of the past.

Links

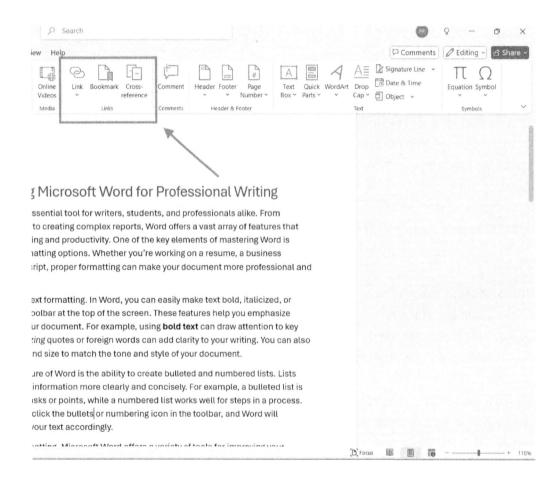

The **Links** section allows you to insert hyperlinks and internal references to facilitate navigation and improve the document's structure.

- **Hyperlink** (Ctrl + K): This command creates a link to a web page, external document, or location within the same document.
- **Bookmark**: Places a bookmark in the document that can be hyperlinked, useful for quickly navigating through long documents.
- **Cross-referencing**: This feature inserts a link to another part of the document, such as tables, figures, or headings, allowing you to reference related items.

Text

This section allows you to insert additional text elements that improve the structure and appearance of the document.

- **Text Box**: An independent text box can be placed anywhere in the document.
- **WordArt**: Inserts decorative text with special effects (shadows, outlines, slews), often used for headings or sections that need to capture attention.
- **Date & Time**: This function adds the current date and time to the document, and there are different formats to choose from.
- **Digital signature**: Inserts a space for the digital signature, which is used to authenticate the document or for official approvals.
- **Object**: This function inserts an external object, such as an Excel sheet or PDF file, that can be embedded in the document.

Symbols

The **Symbols section** helps enter special characters or mathematical equations.

- **Equation**: Inserts a predefined mathematical equation or allows you to create custom equations supporting advanced symbols such as fractions, integrals, and powers.
- **Symbol**: Adds special symbols or characters do not present on the keyboard, such as the copyright symbol (©) or the currency symbol (¥).

Draw

The **Drawing** tab in Microsoft Word allows users to interact with the document more creatively and visually, allowing them to draw freehand directly on the document. This card is handy for those working on touch devices or with a digital pen, such as tablets. It is ideal for quick annotations, sketches, or manual additions that enrich the content. The tools on the **Drawing** tab are intuitive and allow you to convert manual strokes into text or shapes, simplifying the drawing and editing process.

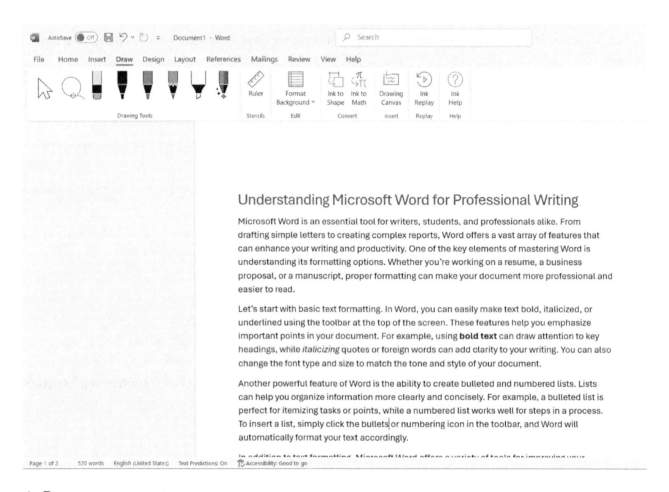

1. Pens

The **Pens** section allows you to select various writing or hand-drawing tools with different styles and colors.
- **Ballpoint pen**: A tool that simulates a ballpoint pen, ideal for writing notes or making precise annotations. You can select various thicknesses and colors for the pen.
- **Fountain pen**: This simulates a fountain pen with softer, more flexible strokes, often used for signatures or decorative strokes.
- **Highlighter**: A tool that allows you to highlight areas of text or drawing with translucent colors. Helpful in emphasizing essential parts of the document.
- **Color and thickness**: You can customize the color and thickness of the stroke for each drawing tool. Colors can be chosen from a predefined palette or customized.

- **Add a new pen**: This option allows you to add new pen styles or highlighters to the toolbar while selecting advanced options such as ink effects.

The pen features in Microsoft Word were introduced about ten years ago. They are primarily designed for tablets and devices with large, touch-sensitive screens. Initially, the goal was to make interacting with documents more intuitive through digital pens, allowing for handwritten notes, highlighting, or marking directly on the text.

Thanks to technological advancements in screen resolution and overall display quality, the pen experience has dramatically improved. Modern devices, equipped with higher-resolution screens and advanced touch and pressure recognition technologies, provide a digital writing experience that closely mimics traditional handwriting. Adding to this are the latest precision-pointing tools and digital pens, offering high sensitivity and accuracy, which make interactions smoother and more natural. The pen section in Microsoft Word has recently been expanded and enhanced, including advanced tools for writing and drawing. Now, users can write and take notes and create sketches or complex annotations directly on Word documents, transforming the application into a fully-fledged platform for creative writing and productivity. These features are designed for those using Word on touch-enabled devices, such as tablets and 2-in-1 computers, and aim to compete with the best drawing and writing apps on the market.

Integrating digital pens with Microsoft Word makes annotating and personalizing documents faster and more intuitive, allowing users to directly interact with the text. Whether highlighting key points, drawing diagrams, or making quick corrections, the pen technology offers a unique user experience. This is especially useful for people working in creative or educational settings, where visual note-taking and dynamic content interaction are essential.

The evolution of pen tools in Word marks a significant advancement for productivity on touch devices. It offers the perfect combination of advanced functionality and ease of use, getting closer to the standards set by the best apps specifically designed for digital drawing and writing.

Ink to Text

The **Ink to Text** feature is an advanced feature that converts manually drawn strokes into digital text.

- **Convert Drawing to Text**: This feature automatically recognizes handwritten words and turns them into editable text. It's beneficial for taking handwritten notes that can be turned into digital text without needing to rewrite.
- **Convert Drawing to Shapes**: This feature converts hand-drawn shapes (such as circles, squares, or arrows) into perfect geometric figures. It is useful for creating precise diagrams or graphs from sketches.

Tires

The **Erasers** section offers tools to easily erase parts of the drawing or entire strokes created manually.

- **Small Eraser**: This tool is ideal for erasing small errors or details, allowing you to correct complex designs without altering the rest of your work.

- **Medium Eraser**: This tool offers an intermediate erase size for removing medium-sized sections without the need to be too precise.
- **Large Eraser**: This tool erases large areas of your drawing in a single step, making it useful for deleting entire strokes or unnecessary sections.
- **Stroke Eraser**: Rather than erasing specific areas, this eraser removes entire drawing strokes, automatically deleting everything created with a single tap or stroke.

Additional Tools

In addition to the essential tools, additional tools may be available on the Drawing tab that supports a more dynamic and rich experience.

- **Ruler**: A digital ruler that can be used to draw straight lines or to measure angles. It can be rotated and moved precisely, making drawing precise diagrams and geometric shapes easy.
- **Edit pens**: This tool allows you to edit saved pen styles in detail, such as changing the color, transparency, or thickness of an existing pen.

Freehand drawing

In addition to the specific tools, the **Drawing** tab supports freehand drawing, especially on touch devices or with digital pens. Users can draw directly on the document, make annotations, or create sketches that remain embedded in the text.

Layout

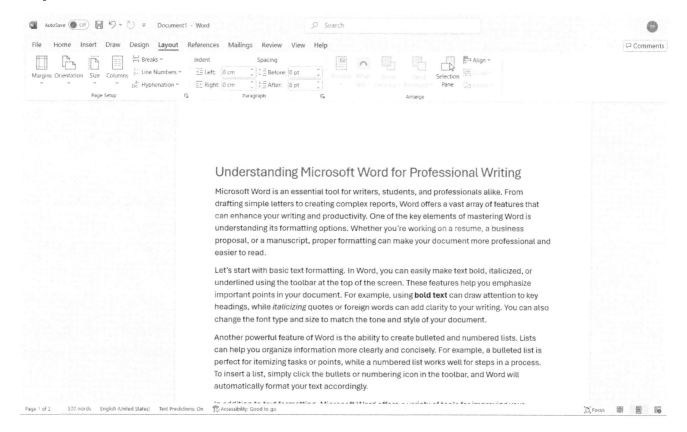

The **Layout** tab in Microsoft Word is critical for controlling your document's overall structure and appearance. You can manage margins, page orientation, paper size, and columns here, ensuring your document is formatted correctly. The features offered by this tab are essential for those working on professional documents, reports, or complex projects, where text and graphic elements must be precise and well-organized.

Page Setup

The **Page Setup section** allows you to define how the document will be displayed and controls essential parameters such as margins and orientation.

- **Margins**: This option adjusts the width of the document's margins (top, bottom, left, right). Predefined options (narrow, normal, wide) are available, or you can customize them manually.
- **Orientation**: Defines the orientation of the document:
    - **Vertical**: The traditional layout, where the page is taller than it is wide.
    - **Landscape**: Flips the page, making it more comprehensive than tall and helpful for wide tables or charts.
- **Size**: Select the page size. The most common options are **A4** (the standard for most documents) and **Letter** (the US standard), but you can choose other sizes or customize one.
- **Columns**: This feature divides text into multiple columns, which is useful for creating documents such as brochures or articles. You can choose the number of columns and their width.

- **Breaks**: Add page breaks, column breaks, or section breaks:
    - **Page break**: Moves the text that follows to a new page.
    - **Column Break**: Moves the text to the next column.
    - **Section Break**: This divides the document into sections, allowing you to apply different formatting (e.g., margins or orientation) for each section.

Paragraph

The **Paragraph** section allows you to control the spacing and indentation of text to improve your document's readability and visual structure.

- **Indent**: Adjusts the indentation of text relative to the document's margins.
    - **Left and Right**: Moves the entire paragraph inward from the left or right margin, which helps create indented text blocks.
    - **First line**: Indent only the first line of the paragraph, typical in narrative or formal writing.
    - **Suspended**: Indents are all paragraph lines except the first one, commonly used in bibliographies.
- **Spacing**: Controls the space before and after paragraphs.
    - **Space before**: Adds extra space before a paragraph, which helps separate text sections.
    - **Space After**: Adds space after the paragraph, improving readability without manually inserting line breaks.
- **Line Spacing**: Defines the space between lines of text within a paragraph, with default options such as single, 1.5 lines, or double. You can also set custom line spacing.

From experience, I believe that setting the page layout, margin size, and spine width (if needed) should be done at the beginning of any project. However, this task is relatively simple today. If you want to keep a particular paper size, specific formatting, or styles from a previous document, copy the original document into a folder and rename it. When you open the document and delete all content, the internal formatting, spacing, fonts, margins, and styles will remain unchanged. This way, you can immediately start working with the desired formatting. This simple trick saves you from setting all the document's general and specific parameters. For those who aren't experts, it can be a significant time-saver.

Arrange

The **Arrange** section controls the position and handling of graphic objects relative to text, such as images, shapes, or tables. It's crucial when working with multimedia content embedded in text.

- **Position**: Defines where to place an object in the document, such as an image or shape.
    - You can select predefined positions, such as aligning the object up, center, or down to the text.
- **Wrap Text**: Manages how the text wraps around the inserted objects, with options such as:
    - **In line with text**: The object behaves like part of the text, moving with it.
    - **Close**: Text flows around the object, following its contours.

- **Above and Below**: Text only flows above or below the object, leaving free space on the sides.
- **Bring Forward**/Backward: Adjusts the order of overlapping objects.
    - **Move Forward**: Moves the selected object on top of the others.
    - **Bring Back**: Moves the object behind other items.
- **Align**: Align multiple selected objects to or to each other in the document's margins, with vertical or horizontal alignment options.
- **Group/Gruppe**: Group various objects to move or resize them together or ungroup them to edit them individually.
- **Rotate**: Rotates an object in different directions or allows free rotation. You can rotate 90° or flip the object horizontally or vertically.

References

The References tab in Microsoft Word is essential for those working on academic, technical, or legal papers. It offers advanced tools for managing citations, bibliographies, indexes, and notes. Using this tab, you can automate the creation of tables of contents, footnotes, and cross-references, ensuring a document that is structured, professional, and easy to navigate. The features in this tab are handy for creating theses, academic papers, reports, and other formal documents.

Table of Contents

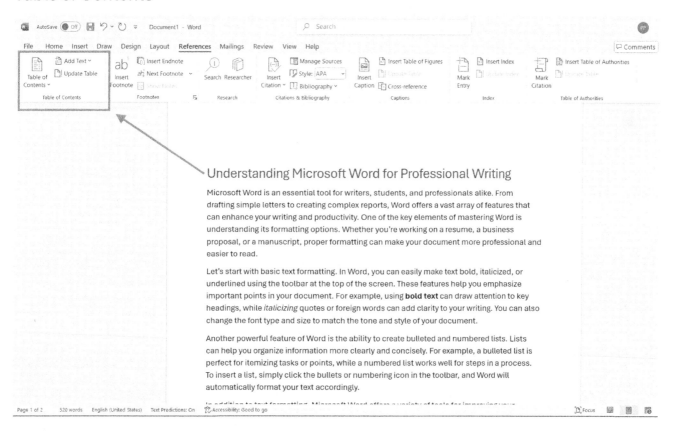

The **Table of Contents section** allows you to create and manage an automatic table of contents for your document based on the heading styles you apply.

- **Auto-Table of Contents**: This tool creates a table of contents that automatically updates based on the document's titles (Heading 1, Heading 2, etc.). You can choose from various pre-made templates.
- **Custom Table** of Contents: This allows you to customize the table of contents by choosing which heading levels to include, how to display page numbers, and other formatting options.
- **Update Table of** Contents: After editing the document, this feature allows you to update the table of contents with the new information, ensuring consistency between the content and the table of contents.

Footnotes

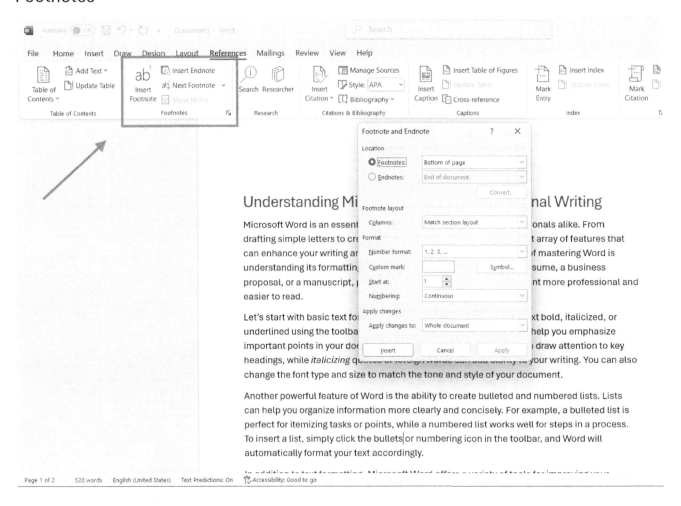

The **Footnotes** section handles the insertion of footnotes or endnotes, often used to add comments, references, or additional information.

- **Insert Footnote**: Insert a footnote at the end of the current page. Notes are automatically numbered.

- **Insert endnote**: Adds a note to the document's or section's end. Again, the notes are numbered automatically.
- **Go to Next/Previous Note**: This allows you to quickly navigate through footnotes or endnotes within the document.
- **Show Notes**: Displays all footnotes or endnotes, allowing for easier management of all annotations.

Be mindful of **footnotes**. Footnotes help readers better navigate your Word document. Besides page numbers, footnotes reference the bibliography or define terms and concepts within the page. However, footnotes also follow the structure of your document's sections. Hence, it's advisable to dedicate a specific, well-formatted section to keep footnotes organized and positioned. Even a tiny error could lead to confusion or a lack of clarity. Therefore, it's best to add them at the end, during the editing or proofreading phase.

Citations and bibliography

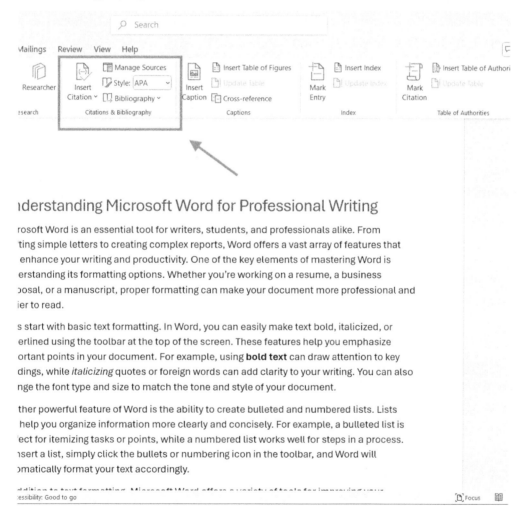

This section is dedicated to managing academic citations and automatically creating bibliographies, with support for different citation styles.

- **Insert Quote**: This allows you to insert a quote into the text. You can choose from a list of previously saved sources or add new ones.
- **Manage Sources**: This opens a panel where you can insert, edit, or delete bibliographic sources. Sources can also be exported or imported, making it simple to use duplicate citations in different documents.
- **Style**: You can select the desired citation style (APA, MLA, Chicago, etc.), automatically adapting the citations and bibliography.
- **Bibliography**: Inserts an automatically generated bibliography based on the sources used in the document. You can choose from several predefined templates.

Captions

The **Captions** section allows you to label and manage captions for images, tables, charts, and other objects, making your document more readable and easier to navigate.

- **Insert caption**: Adds a caption to an image, table, or other object. Captions are automatically numbered, such as "Figure 1" or "Table 1."
- **Insert Figure List**: This function creates an automatic list of figures based on the captions you enter, which is useful for documents with many images or charts.
- **Update Captions**: This feature allows you to update the list of figures or tables if captions change position or numbering, maintaining document consistency.
1. Table of Contents

The **Index** section helps create a detailed index based on specific keywords or concepts in the document.

- **Insert Index**: This function creates an index based on the bookmarks and flagged entries in the document. The index includes the pages on which the keywords appear.
- **Mark entry**: Select a word or phrase in the document and mark it as an entry for the index, adding a specific entry in the summary.
- **Update Index**: After you edit the document, you can update the index to reflect the new positions of critical entries.

Cross-references

The **Cross-Reference feature** allows you to create internal links between parts of your document, making navigating and maintaining consistency between sections easier.

- **Insert Cross Reference**: Adds a link to another part of the document, such as a title, figure, or table. This feature is handy for references within complex documents, such as technical or academic reports.
- **Update cross-references**: If sections change position or number, you can automatically update the cross-references to maintain the document's integrity.

Mailings

The **Letters** tab in Microsoft Word is dedicated to managing **Mail** Merge, a process that allows you to automate the sending of letters, labels, envelopes, or personalized emails to a list of recipients. This tool is essential for those who need to send large amounts of personalized communications efficiently and professionally, such as in marketing campaigns, invitation management, or business correspondence.

Create

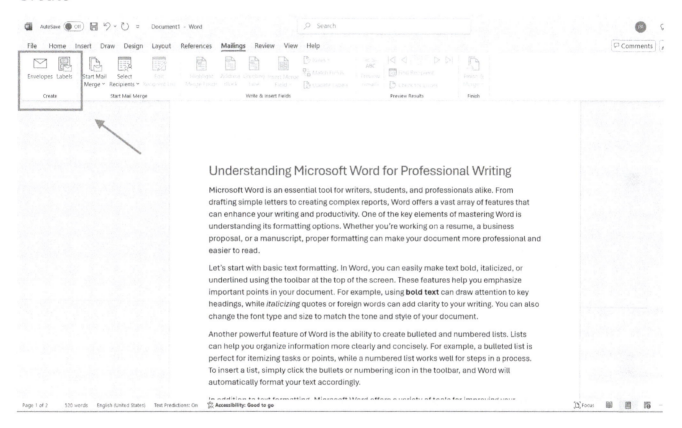

The **Create** section allows you to prepare items such as envelopes, labels, and custom documents for postal mailing.
- **Envelopes**: This opens an interface for creating custom envelopes with predefined addresses. You can choose the envelope size and configure the recipient and sender addresses.
- **Labels**: This allows you to create labels for addresses or other uses. You can choose the format of the labels (e.g., Avery) and link the data for the mail merge to generate customized labels for each recipient.
- **Letter**: Begin the process of creating a personalized letter using mail merge. This function generates letters with variable data (e.g., name, address) taken from a list of recipients.

Start Mail Merge

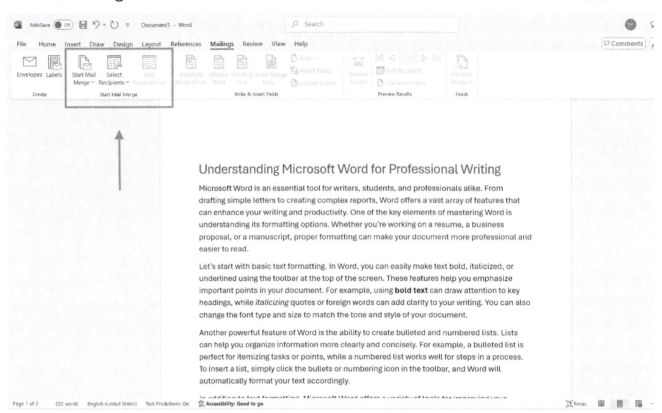

The **Start Mail Merge section** allows you to configure and start the mail merge process, which helps generate customized documents from a single template.
- **Letters**: Set up the current document for creating custom letters, where recipient-specific data will be populated.
- **Email messages**: You can configure the document to send personalized emails in series.
- **Envelopes**: Configure the document to create envelopes, linking addresses from a contact list.
- **Labels**: Start creating labels with custom data.
- **Catalog**: Create a catalog or list with data pulled from a source, such as a database or spreadsheet.

Select recipients

This section is crucial for linking the document to a data source containing recipient information (e.g., names, email addresses, mailing addresses).
- **Type a new list**: Create a new list of recipients directly within Word. A window opens where you can manually enter names and addresses.
- **Use an existing list**: Link the document to an existing list containing recipient data, such as an Excel sheet or Access database.
- **Select from Outlook Contacts**: You can import recipients from your Microsoft Outlook address book, making it simple to send personalized letters or emails to contacts you've already saved.

Insert merge fields

The **Insert Merge Fields** section allows you to customize documents with variable fields that will be filled with recipients' information during the mail merge process.

- **Address Block**: Automatically inserts an entire address block (including name, address, city, etc.) based on the fields selected in the recipient list.
- **Greeting line**: Insert a personalized greeting line, such as "Dear [First Name]" or "Dear [Last Name]."
- **Insert merge field**: This allows you to insert individual fields from the recipient database, such as "First Name," "Last Name," "Address," or any other specific data available.
- **Rules**: Add conditions or rules to the mail merge, such as "If... So..." (e.g., if the customer is a man, use "Dear Mr."; if it is a woman, use "Dear Mrs.").

Preview Results

The **Preview Results** section is essential to check how your custom documents look before completing and sending them.

- **Preview Results**: Turn on the preview, showing how each merge field will be filled with the recipient's data. This allows you to check if everything is correct before finalizing the document.
- **Forward/**Backward: This option allows you to scroll through the various documents customized for each recipient to verify that all the data is correct.
- **Find Recipient**: This allows you to search for a specific recipient within the list and view the custom document for that recipient.

Finalize and merge

This section finalizes the mail merge process, allowing you to create or send the final documents directly.

- **Print Documents**: Prints all custom letters or documents created with mail merge. You can print all documents, just a specific range, or just a specific document.
- Send emails directly to the document, connecting to Outlook's default email account email. **Individual documents**: Create a new document containing all your custom letters or messages so you can make additional edits before printing or sending.

Review

The Review tab in Microsoft Word provides advanced tools for verifying and correcting document content. It is designed to support the review and collaboration process, allowing you to correct errors, manage changes, add comments, and ensure the linguistic quality of the text. These tools are handy in collaborative, academic, or professional work environments where multiple people must review and edit a document.

Spelling and grammar check

The **Spelling and grammar check section** helps you correct your document's spelling, grammar, and style errors.

- **Spelling and grammar** (F7): Starts automatic document review, identifying spelling and grammar errors. The control suggests corrections and allows you to accept or dismiss suggestions.
- **Editor**: An extension of spelling and grammar checking that analyzes the style, clarity, conciseness, and formality of the text. It also provides suggestions for improving the readability and consistency of the document.

Research

The **Search** section provides tools to dive deeper into the meaning of words or find synonyms and definitions.

- **Thesaurus** (Shift + F7): This function offers a list of synonyms for the selected Word, useful for avoiding repetition or finding more appropriate words.
- **Definition**: Quickly look up the meaning of a word using online dictionary sources. Useful for better understanding the context of certain words.

Language

This section manages the language settings of the document and allows you to translate parts of the text.

- **Set Editing Language**: Select the language for spelling and grammar checking so that Word can correctly identify errors based on your chosen language.

- **Translate**: Opens Word's built-in translator, allowing you to translate the entire document or sections of text into other languages.

Advanced grammar checking: Turn grammar checking on or off based on your specific language settings.

Remarks

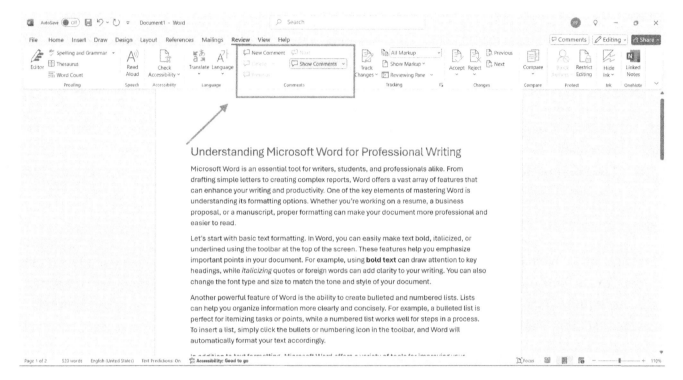

The **Comments** section allows you to add notes to your document without directly changing the content. It is beneficial for collaboration, allowing multiple users to discuss aspects of the text.
- **New Comment**: Adds a comment on a document's word, phrase, or section. Comments are displayed in the margin and identified by the person who made them.
- **Delete**: Removes the selected comment. You can delete all comments at once or one at a time.
- **Previous/Next**: Allows you to navigate through the comments inserted in the document.
- **Show Comments**: Shows or hides comments in the document's margin, allowing for a more precise text display.

Track Changes

The **Track Changes** section is one of the most powerful tools for collaborative work. It allows you to track all changes made to the document.
- **Track Changes**: This activates the mode that tracks all changes made in the document, highlighting them with different colors based on the user who created them.
- **Show for review**: Allows you to view the document in different modes:
    - **All Revision Marks**: Shows all changes made.
    - **Original**: Shows the document in its original form, unedited.

- **Edited**: Shows the final document with all the changes accepted.
- **Accept or Reject Changes**: This option allows you to approve or reject individual changes made by other reviewers. You can do this one at a time or apply the choices to all changes in the document in bulk.

Protection

The **Security** section provides tools to protect your document from unauthorized changes, ensuring only users with the appropriate permissions can make changes.
- **Protect Document**: Opens a menu with options to limit the ability to make changes to the document. You can only allow reviews or restrict editing to specific sections.
- **Restrict Changes**: Set rules that limit changes to reviewers. You can enable only tracked comments or edits, blocking unauthorized edits.
- **Lock permissions**: Protects the document with a password, ensuring that only those who know the password can remove your set restrictions.

View

The View tab in Microsoft Word provides several tools for changing the way a document appears on the screen. These tools do not affect the content of the document but improve its readability and navigation, adapting to the user's preferences or the type of work being done. They're especially useful for switching between different viewing modes, managing the layout of multiple windows, and accessing advanced features like macros.

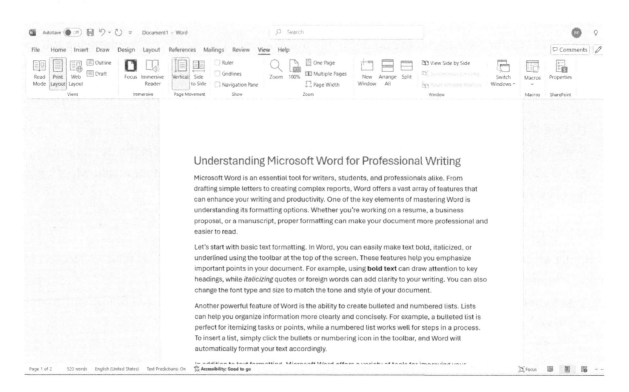

Document views

This section allows you to switch between different display modes optimized for specific purposes.

- **Reading layout**: This layout optimizes the document for on-screen reading by hiding editing tools and showing text in a larger, simpler view. It's ideal for distraction-free content review.
- **Print layout**: This view shows the document as it will appear when printed, with margins, headers, footers, and correct formatting. It is the default view for most users.
- **Web Layout**: Simulates the display of the document as it would appear on a web page. It is useful when working with documents that will be published online or converted to HTML.
- **Draft**: Shows the document in a simplified mode, mainly highlighting the text without displaying complex formatting. It is helpful for quick review or editing of content.

Zoom

The **Zoom** section offers controls to adjust the magnification of the document view without changing the content.

- **Zoom**: This opens a dialog box that allows you to manually select the zoom level, such as 100% or 75%, or to fit the view to one page or multiple pages at once.
- **100%**: Immediately returns the zoom level to 100%, the default view level.
- **One page**: Adapt the view to show a single page on the screen.
- **Two Pages**: This view adapts to show two pages side by side, ideal for comparing consecutive pages in multi-page documents.
- **Page Width**: Adjust the zoom to fit the width of the page to the screen, which is helpful for more comfortable reading and editing.

Window

The **Window** section allows you to manage multiple Word windows at once, making it easy to compare or work on multiple documents simultaneously.

- **New Window**: This option opens a new window of the same document, allowing you to view and edit different parts of the document at once without constantly scrolling up and down.
- **Arrange All**: Automatically arranges all open windows on the screen, allowing you to view multiple documents simultaneously.
- **View Side by Side**: This option shows two documents side by side, making it easy to compare them directly. It is beneficial for reviewing different versions of the same document.
- **Synchronous scrolling**: This feature allows you to scroll through two documents displayed side-by-side simultaneously, synchronizing their movements for easier comparison.
- **Reset Window Position**: Returns side-by-side windows to their original size, which is helpful after manually resizing windows.

Switch Window: Quickly switch between windows if multiple documents or multiple windows of the same document are open.

Macros

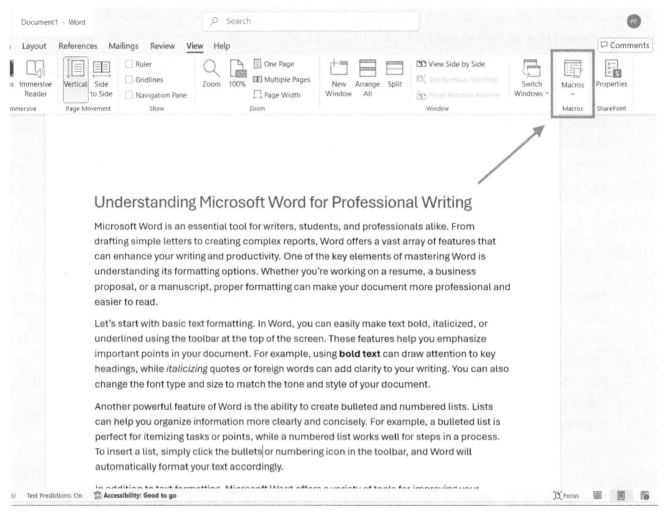

The **Macros** section provides tools for automating repetitive tasks within Word, facilitating complex or time-consuming processes.
- **View** Macros: Opens a list of available macros. A macro is a sequence of commands or actions executed automatically with a single click.
- **Record Macros**: You can record a series of actions in Word to automate them. Once recorded, the macro can be run whenever you want to replicate that series of actions.
- **Use Macro**: Allows you to run a macro that has already been recorded or created, thus automating the process of repeating tasks.

Help

The **Help** tab in Microsoft Word provides support tools and resources to help you find solutions to problems, explore specific features, and get technical assistance. This tab is designed to make the user experience easier and more accessible by providing quick access to Microsoft documentation, online help, and support. It also allows you to provide direct feedback to Microsoft to improve the program.

Search

The **Search** section is a powerful and versatile search bar that allows you to quickly find tools, features, or assistance within Word.

- **Search bar**: The search bar allows you to search for any feature or command within Word. Enter a keyword, and Word will suggest related tools, functions, or documentation. This feature is ideal for quickly finding a feature without manually navigating through tabs.
  - **For example**, If the user wants to change the font size, they can type "font size" in the search bar, and Word will directly show the related option.

Support

The **Support** section provides quick links to online support resources, where you can find solutions to problems or detailed information about specific features.

- **Microsoft Support**: Direct link to Microsoft's official support pages, where you can find help articles, tutorials, and step-by-step guides on how to use the different features of Word.
- **Help & Training**: Access training materials, courses, and step-by-step guides to improve your knowledge of the software. These materials help users learn to use advanced features and solve common problems.

Feedback

The **Feedback** section allows users to send feedback directly to Microsoft to improve the program. It's a valuable tool for communicating issues or developing new ideas for future features.

- **Send Feedback**: This option provides a window where the user can write feedback about Word. You can report technical issues or bugs, request new features, or simply submit feedback about the software.
- **Tell Microsoft what you like**: A subsection to give positive feedback about your experience using Word, which can positively influence the future development of your application.

The **Help** tab is a critical support tool for anyone who uses Microsoft Word. It offers immediate resources to troubleshoot issues, explore new features, and get help. By integrating a powerful search bar, links to online help, and the ability to provide direct feedback, this tab improves the user experience, making Word more accessible and easier to use even for less experienced users.

AI-powered text correction tools

As Microsoft Word continues to evolve into the Office 365 suite, the new features in document proofreading are revolutionizing the way we work. For professionals who use Word daily to draft essential documents, these innovations can mean the difference between a job completed efficiently and one that requires hours of manual review.

Microsoft has recently enhanced Word's proofreading system, going far beyond just checking spelling and grammar. Now, thanks to artificial intelligence, Word can analyze text more deeply, offering suggestions not only on typos but also on complex aspects such as lexicon, syntax, formal register, and conciseness.

Word analyzes the context of the document to provide more appropriate lexical suggestions. For example, suppose Sarah is preparing a formal document for her boss or a client. In that case, Word can suggest more formal alternatives to words or phrases that are too colloquial. This assistance helps maintain a professional and consistent record in every part of the document, improving the communicative impact.

Syntax and Fluency

Another field of improvement is the revision of the syntax. Word's AI doesn't just point out grammatical errors; it suggests ways to make sentences smoother and more understandable. This means that Sarah can receive advice on how to restructure a sentence that is too complex or improve the clarity of the message she is trying to communicate, reducing the risk of misunderstandings or confusion.

One of the biggest challenges for professional paper writers is keeping the text concise and to the point. Word's artificial intelligence also helps with this, pointing out redundant or too-long sentences and suggesting shorter and more direct alternatives. This not only reduces the reading time for recipients but also increases the effectiveness of the message.

Customizing Suggestions

These personalized tips are a real advantage for Sarah, who is often short on time and wants to learn quickly. Microsoft Word learns from your writing style and previous choices, creating corrections that fit your preferences. This makes the proofreading process even faster and more effective, eliminating the need to manually review each tip.

Thanks to these new artificial intelligence features, Word is no longer just a writing tool but a real assistant that helps improve the quality of documents. This means you can work safer and more efficiently, saving valuable time and improving overall productivity.

These innovations make Word a tool that not only corrects errors but also helps professionals achieve a new level of accuracy and professionalism in their documents.

Advanced Tips

Microsoft Word is packed with advanced features that, when used correctly, can make your workflow much more efficient and productive. Knowing shortcut commands, learning how to manage macros, or making the best use of search and replace functions saves you time and gets professional results faster and easier. In this paragraph, we'll explore some **advanced tips** to optimize your use of Microsoft Word and improve your productivity.

1. Shortcut commands to speed up your workflow

One of the best ways to save time while using Word is to learn and use shortcut **commands**(shortcuts). Instead of navigating through the menus and Ribbon options, you can perform numerous tasks with simple key combinations, making your work faster and more efficient.

Here are some of the most helpful shortcut commands:

- **Ctrl + C:** Copy
- **Ctrl + V**: Paste
- **Ctrl + X**: Cut
- **Ctrl + Z**: Undo
- **Ctrl + Y**: Repeat

- **Ctrl + B**: Bold
- **Ctrl + I**: Italic
- **Ctrl + U**: Underlined
- Ctrl + F: Find
- **Ctrl + H**: Find and replace

These are just a few basic commands. Still, Word offers plenty of other key combinations that can simplify your experience. By using these commands regularly, you can perform everyday tasks in seconds.

2. Using Macros to Automate Repetitive Tasks

Macros are among the most powerful tools in Word for advanced users. A macro is a sequence of commands and operations that can be recorded and then run automatically whenever needed. This is especially useful when **repetitive tasks**, such as formatting specific documents, inserting predefined text, or applying a variety of structural changes to a document, need to be performed.

To create a macro:

- Go to the "View" tab and select "Macros," then "Record Macros."
- Name your macro and start recording the actions you want to automate.
- Once the recording is complete, you can assign the macro to a Ribbon button or keyboard shortcut to run it quickly.

Using macros allows you to save huge amounts of time on tasks that would otherwise require many manual operations while also reducing the risk of errors.

Advanced Find and Replace

We've already mentioned the **Find and Replace** functionality. Still, some advanced options can make this tool even more powerful. For example, you can use **wildcards** to search for and replace complex text patterns or fix formatting errors that affect multiple parts of the document.

Here are some advanced features:

- **Find and replace formatting**: You can search for text with specific formatting and replace it with another text formatted differently. For example, you can find all words in bold and change them to italics or replace a particular combination of characters with a different color.
- **Wildcards**: Wildcards allow you to search for text patterns. For example, you can search for all words that begin with a particular letter or contain a certain number of characters.

These features are handy when working on long, complex documents and applying changes at scale.

Creating Custom Styles

Suppose you frequently work with documents that require specific formatting. In that case, you can **create custom styles** to quickly apply the same settings to headings, subheadings, paragraphs, and other

47

document sections. Custom styles allow you to format your document consistently, saving time and ensuring a consistent look throughout your text.

To create a custom style:

- Go to the "Home" tab and select "Styles."
- Click "New Style" to configure the font, color, spacing, and other formatting options.
- Save the style; it will be available in any document.

Once created, custom styles can be applied with the click of a button. Suppose you decide to change the style later. In that case, all document sections that use that style will be updated automatically.

5. Use fields to automate parts of the document

Fields in Word are placeholders that can be automatically filled with data such as page numbers, dates, file names, or other variable information. Fields are beneficial for automating repetitive parts of a document and keeping it up to date without manual intervention.

Here are some examples of applicable fields:

- **Page number**: Inserts page numbers that automatically update as the document grows.
- **Date & Time**: You can enter a date that automatically updates when the document is opened.
- **Document Title**: Inserts the file title or other information from the document's metadata.

To insert a field:

- Go to the "Insert" tab and select "Field" in the "Text" group.
- Choose the type of field you want to insert, and Word will automatically generate it.

Using fields allows you to create dynamic documents that always stay up to date without additional manual intervention.

Finally, when working with sensitive or shared documents, you may need to **protect the document** to prevent unauthorized changes. Microsoft Word offers several file protection options, such as setting passwords or **restricting changes**.

To protect a document:

1. Go to the "File" tab and select "Protect Document".
2. You can choose the option you want, such as setting a password, allowing only reading, or restricting changes to specific parts of the document.

This feature is critical when you need to share important documents and want to ensure that the content remains intact and secure.

4. Microsoft Excel 2025

Microsoft Excel 2025 is an essential tool for anyone who works with data professionally and personally. Excel offers a powerful and versatile solution with a wide range of capabilities ranging from simple data organization to complex, automated analysis. In this chapter, we'll explore the key features of Excel 2025, from the basics of layout and customization to the advanced use of formulas and analysis tools. Whether you are a beginner or an experienced user, Excel is a tool that can significantly improve productivity and efficiency in your daily work.

Introduction to Excel 2025

Microsoft Excel 2025 represents a further step forward in the landscape of tools for managing, organizing, and analyzing data. Since its first introduction, Excel has become central to the daily operations of millions of users worldwide, thanks to its versatility and power. The new 2025 version introduces innovative features that make it even easier to manage large volumes of data, analyze it and draw meaningful conclusions, making Excel an essential tool not only for those working in finance or accounting but also for those involved in business management, research, marketing, and many other sectors.

Why learn Excel? Benefits and practical applications

Excel is widely used for various tasks, ranging from managing your personal budget to creating complex business financial models. One of the main reasons you should learn Excel is its ability to **automate repetitive tasks**, making it easier to work on large datasets and reducing the time it takes to perform calculations or update information. Excel also allows you **to visualize your data** clearly and understandably, thanks to charts, pivot tables, and other visualization tools.

Advanced users appreciate Excel's flexibility and ability to be customized to meet their specific needs. You can create custom spreadsheets, use advanced formulas to perform complex analysis, and even integrate Excel with other Microsoft Office applications or third-party software. This makes Excel a practical tool that can be applied to almost any professional and personal situation.

Key Features and Uses

Excel 2025 retains all the core features that have made the platform popular. Still, it also introduces some **new features** that further improve user experience and work efficiency. These include deeper integration with **Power Query** for retrieving data from external sources, **automated analysis** tools to identify trends and anomalies in datasets, and new formatting options that allow you to create professional documents in just a few clicks.

In addition, Excel 2025 offers significant improvements in **collaboration**. With tighter integration with **Microsoft Teams** and **OneDrive**, you can work on the same file simultaneously with other people, with real-time updates that allow everyone on your team to access and edit data seamlessly. This ability to work in synergy dramatically improves productivity. It reduces the risk of errors due to out-of-sync versions of the file.

Home

The **Home** tab in Excel is the starting point for most worksheet formatting and management. You can find all the essential tools to manipulate data, apply formatting, and manage cells here. The tab is organized into sections that allow you to quickly edit the sheet's contents.

Clipboard

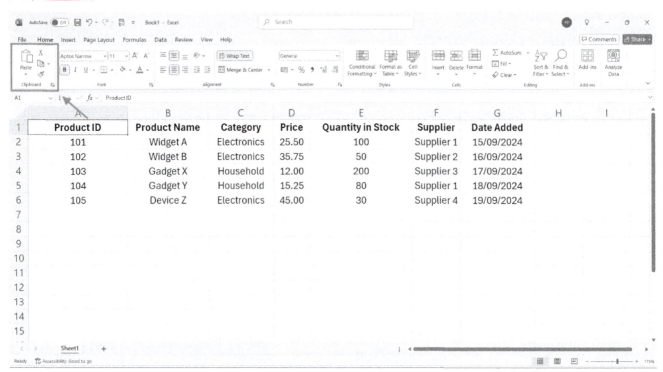

- **Copy** (Ctrl + C): Duplicates the selected content to the clipboard.
- **Cut** (Ctrl + X): Removes the selected content and copies it to the clipboard.
- **Paste** (Ctrl + V): Insert copied or cut content from the clipboard.
- **Paste Special**: You can paste specific content, such as only values, formatting, or formulas.

Character

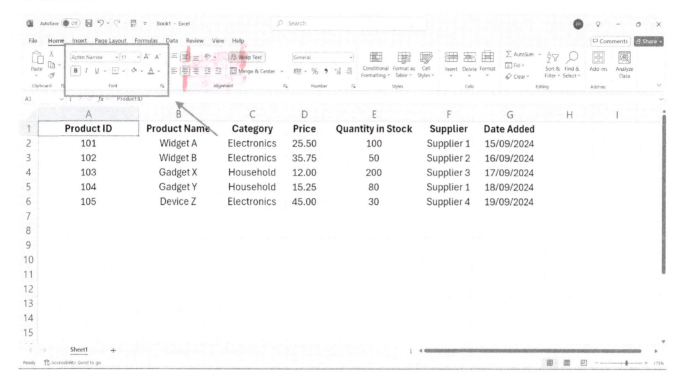

- **Font**: Change the font of the text in the cells.
- **Font size**: Change the size of the text.
- **Bold** (Ctrl + B), **Italic** (Ctrl + I), **Underline** (Ctrl + U): Apply formatting to the text.
- **Font Color**: Change the color of the text.
- **Cell Fill**: Change the background of selected cells.

Alignment

- **Align Left, Center, Right**: Defines text alignment in cells.
- **Wrap Text**: Allows text to go on multiple lines within the same cell.
- **Merge and Center**: Combine various cells into one and center the content.

Number

- **Number Format**: Change the format of the cells, choosing from formats such as number, currency, date, percentage, etc.
- **Increase/Decrease Decimals**: Increase or decrease the decimals shown for the selected numbers.

Styles

- **Conditional formatting**: This method applies automatic formatting to cells based on specific criteria (e.g., highlighting values above a certain number).
- **Cell styles**: Apply default formatting to cells, such as headings, titles, or custom styles.

Cells

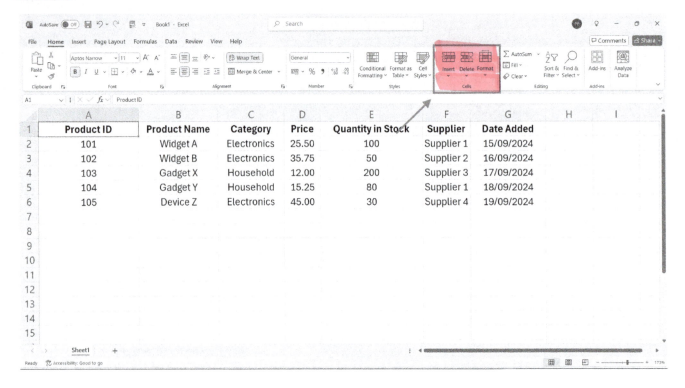

- **Insert**: Inserts new rows, columns, or cells.
- **Delete**: Removes rows, columns, or cells.
- **Format**: Manages row and column sizes, cell protection, and visibility (hide or show rows and columns).

Edit

- **AutoSum**: Adds an auto sum function for numbers in selected cells.
- **Fill**: Allows you to automatically fill cells with a series of numbers, dates, or formulas.
- **Sorting and filtering**: Sort data in ascending or descending order and apply filters to show only relevant data.
- **Search and Select**: Find or replace text, numbers, or formulas in cells.

Insert

Calculator

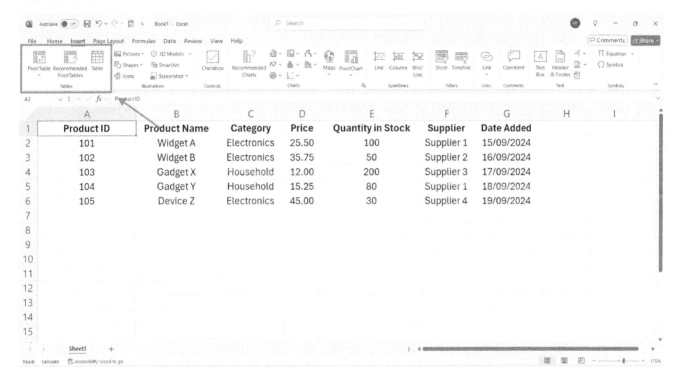

Tables are essential for organizing data and working with it in a structured way.

- **Table**: Allows you to transform a range of cells into a structured table with headers, rows, and columns. Tables make it easy to automatically sort, filter, and format data.
- **Pivot Table**: A powerful tool for data analysis. Create a pivot table that dynamically summarizes, analyzes, and visualizes large amounts of data.
- **PivotChart**: This tool creates a chart based on the data from a pivot table, which is useful for graphically displaying the results of data analysis.

The use of tables in Excel can often serve a more visual than functional purpose, especially when you've become comfortable with the software and are dealing with files containing a vast number of columns and rows. One simple trick that can make a big difference is creating a new worksheet at the bottom left and only including the columns and rows relevant to you, pulled from the original sheets. This way, you can avoid creating a table just for organizing data and, instead, work directly within the spreadsheet, applying the necessary formulas or calculations to quickly and accurately display the data you're interested in.

Working in the original file, filled with data often irrelevant to your specific analysis, and setting up a table to get a clearer view can become frustrating. It can also waste valuable time. Creating a table or focusing on details like choosing the right font or aligning the cells correctly provides a neat and organized view of the data. Still, isolating specific data points or making statistical predictions are only sometimes necessary.

However, there are situations where the visual aspect is crucial. If you're renting your work to your boss or clients or preparing a report that needs to be visually appealing and easy to understand, aesthetics matter. In these cases, paying attention to the graphical layout isn't about appearances—it's about making the data more accessible and understandable. That said, from my experience, paying attention to the graphics can take up a lot of time. Creating a visually polished presentation with well-formatted tables, harmonious colors, and neatly arranged data might seem secondary to the content. Still, it often becomes crucial for effectively conveying the information.

So, my advice is this: when you're looking to write for yourself or perform a quick analysis, prioritize simplicity and focus on Excel's Executive Technical functions. But when you need to present your work, take the extra time to make it visually appealing—know that this step will take additional time. It's up to you to strike the right balance between functionality and visual presentation.

Graphs

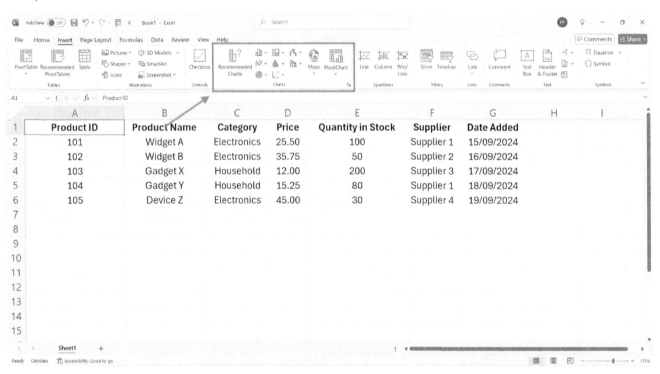

The **Charts** section is one of the most essential tools for data visualization. It allows you to create graphical representations that make your data more understandable.

- **Recommended chart**: Suggests the most suitable chart type based on the selected data. It's a great place to start for those unsure which charts to choose.
- **Standard charts**: This tool allows you to create various types of charts, such as columns, bars, lines, pies, areas, and others. Each chart is useful for displaying data differently.
- **Combo charts** allow you to combine two or more chart types into the same chart for a more complex visualization of your data.
- **Waterfall and stock chart**: It includes specific charts such as the waterfall chart, which helps display the cumulative trend of a series of values, and stock charts to represent financial data.

Charts are one of Excel's most influential and valuable features. Through this, we can obtain an immediate visual representation of a data set, allowing us to quickly understand the trend of a particular parameter, function, or phenomenon. Charts help us visualize historical data and are crucial for making forecasts and projections, helping us understand how a specific parameter might evolve over time and providing critical insights for future decision-making.

Mastering charts is, therefore, one of the essential skills for anyone who uses Excel, as it allows you to transform raw data into clear, easy-to-interpret, and communicable visual information. Whether you're analyzing your data, tracking company growth, or conducting statistical analyses, charts make these processes faster and more intuitive. Their importance is crucial, especially when communicating results effectively to colleagues, superiors, or clients, where clarity and presentation make a difference.

In the bonus material provided in this book, I will also include some simple yet effective tricks to help you create visually appealing charts for Excel's main Excel spreadsheet. Creating a good chart that accurately represents values and is structured clearly and understandably can make the difference between presenting good work and outstanding work. A well-made chart highlights the critical points of your work and captures the viewer's attention. Data analysis is more engaging and professional.

Illustrations

The **Illustrations** section allows you to insert images and other graphics into your spreadsheet, improving its visual appeal and making your data easier to understand.

- **Images**: Allows you to insert pictures from your computer or online sources to enrich your document.
- **Online images**: Search for and insert images directly from web sources like Bing or OneDrive.
- **Shapes**: This option adds predefined shapes (rectangles, arrows, ovals, etc.) that can be used to create diagrams or emphasize specific information.
- **Icons**: This function inserts predefined icons to enhance the presentation of the worksheet, especially useful for making the information more visual and immediate.
- **SmartArt**: Inserts graphics to visually represent processes, hierarchies, or cycles. Useful for complex diagrams.

Add-ons

Add-ins offer extensions to enhance Excel's functionality, allowing you to automate processes or connect to external tools.

- **Add-ins**: This allows you to install and manage additional tools that extend Excel's capabilities. You can add them directly from the Microsoft Store or import them from other sources.

Sparkline Chart Thumbnails

Sparklines are small charts located within a single cell. They are used to visualize trends or changes in data.

- **Line, Column, Win/Loss**: These charts are displayed within cells and offer a quick way to view trends directly next to the data. They are ideal for displaying small time series or comparisons between values.

Filters

Interactive filters allow you to select and visualize data dynamically.

- **Slicer**: Inserts an interactive filter that allows you to filter the data of a table or pivot table visually, selecting criteria directly from the worksheet.
- **Timeline**: Create a time-scrolling filter to analyze a pivot table's data based on a timeline, such as specific dates or months.

Links

The **Links** section allows you to add hyperlinks and bookmarks to improve navigation or link external data.
- **Hyperlink**: Insert a link to a web page, another file, or a specific location within the worksheet.
1. Text

This section allows you to insert additional or unique text elements into your spreadsheet.
- **Text Box**: An independent text box can be placed anywhere on the worksheet.
- **Header and Footer**: Inserts headers and footers to add information such as file name, page number, or date to each printed page.

WordArt allows you to insert decorative text with special effects or sound for headings or sections that need to catch your attention.

Symbols

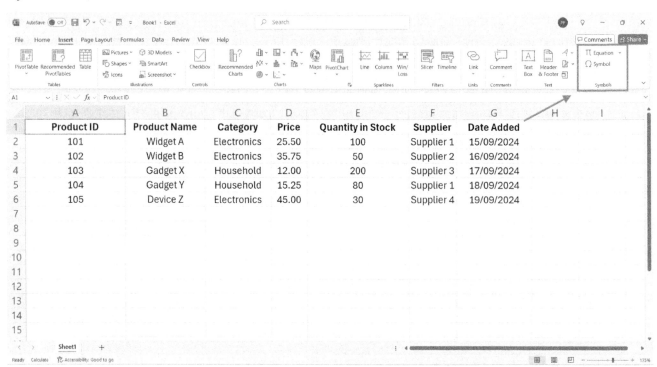

This section allows you to enter special characters or symbols that are not present on the keyboard.
- **Equation**: Inserts predefined mathematical equations or allows you to create custom equations.
- **Symbol**: You can insert special symbols such as monetary characters, percent signs, or accented letters.

Draw

The **Drawing** tab in Excel is primarily designed for users who use touch devices, such as tablets or iPads. This tab allows you to draw freehand directly in the worksheet using digital pens or fingers. It's beneficial for making quick annotations or highlighting information while working on the go.

Key features:
- **Pens**: Allows you to choose between different types of pens and colors to draw or highlight specific areas of the paper.
- **Eraser**: Erases drawn strokes.

- **Ink to Text**: Converts manual drawing into recognizable text.
- **Pen Editing**: Offers the ability to select or edit cells and data using the pen.

While this tab can be useful for quick editing on touch devices, **Excel is** most powerful on **a desktop** or **web browser**, where it offers more advanced features for data management and analysis.

Page Layout

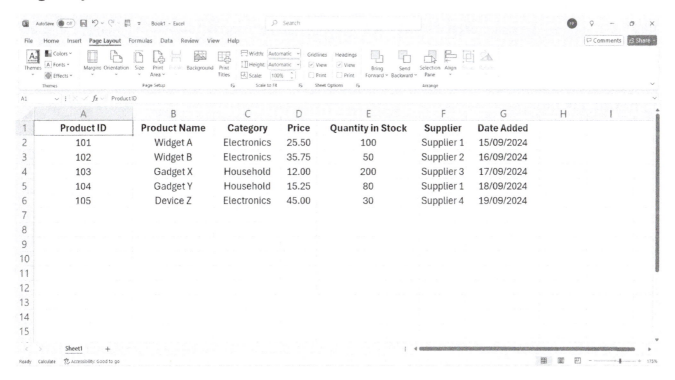

The **Page Layout** tab in Excel is mainly used to manage the appearance of the worksheet, especially in preparation for printing. Here, you will find tools to adjust margins, orientation, and paper size and options to split data across multiple pages. Although print usage has declined with the rise of the cloud and digital sharing, these features remain useful for creating well-formatted versions of documents for printing or exporting to PDF.

Key features:
- **Margins**: Set page margins.
- **Orientation**: Select the page layout between portrait and landscape.
- **Size**: Change the size of the paper (A4, Letter, etc.).
- **Print Area**: Defines the part of the sheet to be printed.
- **Breaks**: Adds page breaks to control where a new page begins.
- **Background**: Insert a custom background into the worksheet (for viewing only, not for printing).
- **Print titles**: Repeats specific rows or columns on each printed page, useful for long tables.

While these features are losing their focus thanks to **cloud** sharing, they are still necessary for those who need to print or create files for physical distribution or static formats.

Formulas

The **Formulas** tab in Excel is undoubtedly one of the most powerful and widely used, essential for taking full advantage of Excel's data analysis and management tool capabilities. This tab gives you access to a wide range of functions and tools for mathematical, statistical, logical, financial calculations and much more. Formulas and functions make Excel an indispensable tool for working with large amounts of data, performing complex calculations, and automating repetitive processes.

This tab groups all the main functions that Excel offers, allowing the user to enter and manage formulas efficiently and organized. The **Formulas tab** is divided into several sections, each dedicated to a different type of function or operation.

Function Library

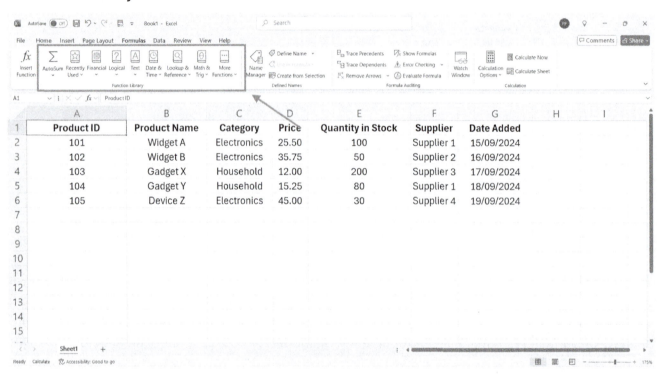

The **Feature Library section** is the heart of the **Formulas** tab, where all the features are categorized. This breakdown makes it easy to find the proper function for the task you need to perform.

- **Mathematical and trigonometric functions**: It contains functions for complex calculations such as sum, mean, product, square roots, powers, and other mathematical operations. For example:
  - **SUM**: Adds all the specified numbers.
  - **PRODUCT:** Multiply the specified numbers.
  - **POWER**: Raises a number to a specific power.
  - **SIN, COS, TAN:** Trigonometric functions for geometric calculations.
- **Logical functions**: Manage operations based on logical conditions and criteria, allowing decisions to be made within Excel.

- **IF**: Performs an operation based on a condition (if true, performs one action; if false, performs another).
  - **E**: Check if all the specified conditions are proper.
  - **O**: Check if at least one of the specified conditions is true.
  - **NON:** Reverses the logical value of a condition (true becomes false and vice versa).
- **Text functions**: Allow you to manipulate text strings. They are helpful for formatting, combining, or editing text within cells.
  - **CHAIN** or **JOIN. TEXT**: Combines the contents of two or more cells into one.
  - **LEFT, RIGHT, STRING. EXTRACT: Extracts** portions of text from a cell.
  - **UPPERCASE, LOWERCASE**: Converts text to uppercase or lowercase.
- **Date and time functions**: Manage and manipulate dates and times, allowing you to perform calculations over time intervals.
  - **TODAY**: Enters the current date.
  - **NOW**: Enters the current date and time.
  - **DATE:** Create a date from numbers by year, month, and day.
  - **DAY. BUSINESS:** Calculate a working date from a start date and several working days, excluding weekends and holidays.
- **Search and reference functions** allow you to search and retrieve data within the sheet or multiple worksheets.
  - **SEARCH. VERT: This function looks** for a value in a column and returns related data from the same row but from a different column.
  - **INDEX:** Returns the value of a cell based on the specified coordinates.
  - **COMPARE: Searches** for a value in a range of cells and returns the relative position.
- **Financial functions**: Useful for calculations such as depreciation, interest rates, payments, and investments.
  - **TIR**: Calculates the internal rate of return for a cash-flow-based investment.
  - **NPV**: Calculates the net present value of a discounted cash flow at a given interest rate.
  - **INSTALLMENT**: Calculate the installment of a loan based on interest rate, number of periods, and loan amount.

Define names

This section is designed to work with **defined names**, which makes it easier to manage and interpret formulas.

Defined Name: This gives a name to a range of cells or a single cell, allowing that name to be used in formulas instead of references such as "A1." It is beneficial for increasing the clarity and readability of formulas.

Name Manager: This button opens a window to view, edit, or delete the names defined in the worksheet.

Formula Checker

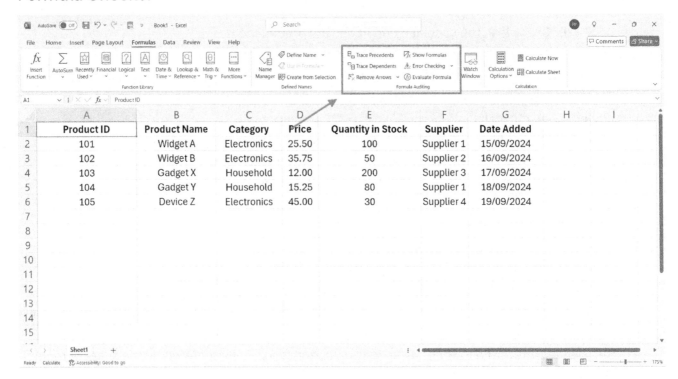

This section helps you verify and correct the formulas in your spreadsheet, identifying errors and ensuring the calculations are correct.

- **Check Formulas** allows you to see a formula's calculation path and understand how operations are performed. This can be useful for identifying errors or anomalies.
- **Show Formulas**: This shows formulas in cells instead of results, which is helpful when reviewing and editing formulas in your worksheet.
- **Evaluate Formula**: This tool allows you to check the execution of a complex formula step by step to identify problems or errors.
- **Check for errors**: Highlights errors in formulas, such as incorrect references or blank cells, and suggests corrections.

Calculation

Excel lets you choose how and when to calculate formula results.

- **Calculation options**: You can set Excel to automatic calculation mode (Excel updates formula results whenever data changes) or manual (Excel updates only when required, valid for complex worksheets).
- **Calculate Now**: Performs an immediate calculation of all formulas in the sheet.
- **Calculate Sheet**: Calculate only the formulas in the active worksheet.

Date

The **Data** tab in Excel is one of the most powerful tools for managing, organizing, and analyzing data. This tab allows you to manipulate large data sets, connect to external sources, apply advanced filters, and use analytics tools to make informed decisions. With the ability to import, transform, and analyze complex data, the **Data tab** is indispensable for those working with financial reports, databases, or large amounts of information.

In this tab, you'll find features that allow you to get and connect data from external sources, sort, and filter in an advanced way, manage duplicate data, and apply complex analysis tools such as **data validation**, **grouping**, and **predictions**.

Get & Transform Data

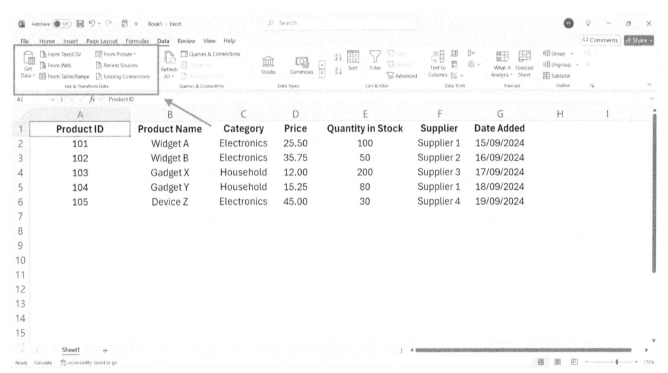

This section is dedicated to importing and transforming data from different sources using Power Query, an advanced tool for connecting, transforming, and modeling data.

- **Get Data** allows you to import data from external sources such as Excel files, CSV files, SQL Server databases, web services, and more. This tool allows you to integrate information from different sources into the worksheet.
- **From table/range**: This connects to a table or range of cells already in the worksheet and allows you to transform the data with Power Query. You can filter, restructure, or model data without changing the original.
- **Query Editor**: Opens the Power Query Editor, which allows you to apply transformations to imported data, such as cleaning, filtering, sorting, and merging datasets.

These tools are especially useful for managing **large volumes of data** from different sources and automating cleaning and organization processes.

In most cases, third-party software programs analyze a series of data and usually export all values in CSV format. In this tab, you can upload CSV data to our spreadsheet.

Range and connections

This section allows you to manage the linked data and the connections between the worksheet and other data sources.

- **Renew All**: Updates all data imported from external sources (such as database-linked tables) to reflect any changes made to the original source.

Connections: Opens a panel that shows all active data connections in the spreadsheet, allowing you to manage or update them.

Sorting and filtering

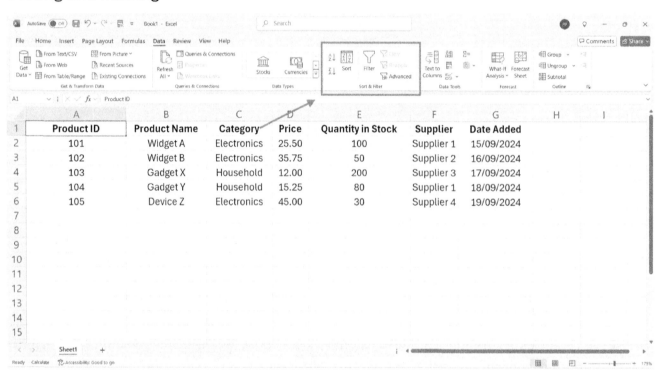

The **Sorting and filtering** section is crucial for organizing and filtering data, especially when working with large amounts of information.

- **Sort A-Z** or **Sort Z-A**: This sorting method sorts the data in ascending or descending order respectively. It is used to sort alphabetical, numeric, or date data.
- **Custom Sorting**: This option allows you to apply sorting based on custom criteria, such as multiple sorting columns or the use of specific colors.
- **Filter**: Adds filters to the worksheet, allowing you to view only rows that meet specific criteria. Filters can be applied to numbers, texts, dates, and even cell colors.

- **Advanced filtering**: Allows you to apply more complex filter criteria than the standard ones. It is useful when multiple or formula-based conditions need to be used.
- **Remove Duplicates**: This feature lets you delete duplicate data from a specific cell range or column, keeping only the unique information.

Data Tools

Data Tools offers advanced tools for data validation, removal, and structuring.
- **Text to columns**: This function divides the contents of a column into multiple columns based on a delimiter (such as commas or spaces). It's beneficial when importing data from external sources such as CSV files or delimiter-separated texts.
- **Group**: Allows you to group data based on time criteria (e.g., days, months, years) or other custom criteria. It's beneficial in pivot tables for aggregating data.
- **Data Validation**: Set rules about the data that can be inserted into a cell. For example, you can limit input to whole numbers, values within a specific range, or choose values from a drop-down list.
- **Consolidate**: Combine data from different ranges or sheets into a single table, summarizing it based on functions such as sum, average, or count.
- **Relationships**: Creates and manages relationships between tables, like relational databases. Relationships make it easier to analyze data in PivotTables, which uses multiple tables.

Forecasts

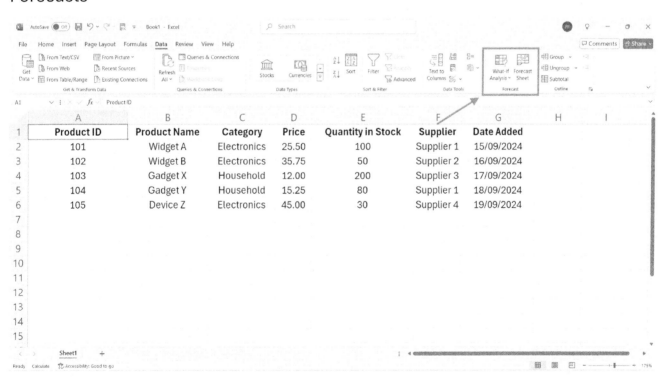

The **Forecasts section** allows you to make estimates and predictive analyses based on historical data, a valuable tool for those in financial or business planning sectors.

- **Forecast sheet**: This function creates a forecast sheet based on time data. Excel automatically generates a future prediction based on historical trends and displays the results with a line chart.
- **Data table**: This allows you to analyze how changes in two variables affect the outcome of a formula, such as in financial models or scenario analysis.

Data Analysis

Excel also offers advanced data analysis tools for complex statistical or economic calculations.

- **What-if analysis**: Allows you to conduct simulations or scenario analysis to predict the impact of changes in data or operating conditions. Includes:
    - **Goal** Lookup: Determines which input value needs to be changed to get a given result in a formula.
    - **Scenarios**: This tool allows you to create and compare different scenarios to analyze how changes in data affect the end results.
    - **Data tables**: Create tables that show the result of a formula for different input values.

Review

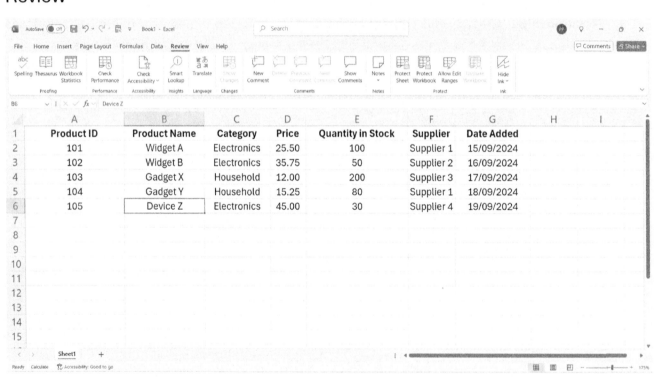

The **Review** tab in Excel is critical for those who need to collaborate with others on the same file and ensure the quality and accuracy of the data. This tab provides tools for reviewing, spelling, commenting, protecting data, and tracking changes. The features on this tab are designed to facilitate collaborative review and help users maintain data integrity and security in spreadsheets.

Below is a detailed description of the main sections of the **Review tab** and their features:

Spell check

This section provides tools to check spelling and correct errors in worksheets.

- **Spelling** (F7): Starts spell checking on the current sheet or the entire document, finding and suggesting corrections for spelling mistakes. Excel checks only textual words and doesn't affect formulas or numeric values.

Accessibility

The **Accessibility** section is designed to help make the spreadsheet easier for users with disabilities to read and navigate.

- **Accessibility Checker**: This tool checks your document for accessibility issues, such as using colors or formats that may be difficult to read. It offers tips to improve accessibility and make the sheet more inclusive.

Translation

This section allows you to translate text within the spreadsheet, making it easier for users of different languages to collaborate.

- **Translate**: This button opens the translation panel, where you can select a target language and translate words or phrases directly in the spreadsheet. This tool uses the Microsoft translation engine and can translate words or entire paragraphs.

Remarks

The **Comments section** allows you to add notes without directly changing the sheet's contents, which is useful for discussions, suggestions, or reviews.

- **New Comment**: This function adds a comment to a selected cell. Comments appear as small icons in the cell and are linked to conversations between collaborators.
- **Reply to comment**: This feature allows you to reply to comments from other users by creating a discussion thread within the document.
- **Delete**: Removes the selected comment. You can delete a single comment or all comments in the worksheet.
- **Previous/Next**: You can navigate through comments, allowing you to easily view and manage all comments in the document.

Notes

Notes are a simpler version of comments, used for quick annotations without a conversation system.

- **New Note**: This function inserts a text note that remains linked to a cell without the complexity of modern comments. Notes appear as simple text boxes and do not create conversation threads.
- **Show Notes**: This option allows you to view all the notes in the worksheet in a consolidated view, allowing you to review and edit them quickly.

Protection

The **Security** section is critical to safeguarding data and limiting unauthorized spreadsheet changes.

- **Protect Sheet**: Adds a password to prevent changes to specific cells or the entire sheet. You can define precisely what operations are allowed, such as editing data, inserting rows and columns, or formatting cells.
- **Protect Workbook**: This option protects the entire workbook to prevent it from being rearranged, such as adding or deleting sheets. It is useful when you want to ensure that the file structure remains the same.
- **Allow Editing Ranges**: Allows you to define specific ranges in the worksheet that can be edited by some users, even if the rest of the sheet is protected. You can assign different passwords to different ranges.
- **Protect and share workbook**: Protect the file and share it with others, keeping a record of all changes made.

Track Changes

This section monitors all changes made to the spreadsheet, keeping track of revisions and making it easy to compare different versions.

- **Highlight Changes**: This section highlights all changes made to the spreadsheet since the last revision. Changes are displayed with markers that show who made them and when.
- **Accept/Reject Changes**: Review your changes and decide which ones to accept or reject. This is useful when working with multiple collaborators and wanting to maintain ultimate control over the data.

Share Workbook: This allows multiple users to work on the same file simultaneously, keeping track of all changes centrally.

View

The **View** tab in Excel is designed to optimize the user experience in managing the worksheet. It allows you to adjust how you view it, the layout, and how you navigate the document. This tab is handy when working on large and complex spreadsheets, as it allows you to customize the interface to make it easier to check and analyze your data. With tools such as zooming, different viewing modes, and window management, users can better focus on relevant information and have more precise control over the layout.

Workbook Views

This section allows you to switch between different display modes, each designed to meet specific needs, such as working on a print layout or simply sketching data.
- **Standard**: The default view of Excel is ideal for editing and viewing data in your worksheet.
- **Page layout**: This shows the worksheet as it will appear when printed, including margins, headers, footers, and page breaks. It is useful for checking and adjusting the appearance of the document before printing.
- **Page Break Preview**: This shows the worksheet with a layout highlighting where page breaks will be placed. You can edit or move breaks for better print organization.

Show

The **Show** section allows you to customize which elements of your worksheet to display, making it easier to view large datasets or hide unnecessary information.
- **Rulers**: Enables or disables rulers that measure the margins of the paper. These rulers are especially useful in **Page Layout** mode for precisely positioning elements.
- **Grid Lines**: Shows or hides separator lines between cells, improving the visual appearance of the sheet or focusing attention on specific elements.
- **Titles**: Toggle the display of row and column headings (such as A, B, and C for columns, and 1, 2, and 3 for rows), making it easier to navigate between cells.
- **Formula bar**: Shows or hides the formula bar, which is useful when working with many formulas or when you want a cleaner interface.

- **Dialog**: Toggle the pane on or off to manage hidden rows or columns.

Zoom

This section offers tools to adjust the worksheet's magnification level, improving readability and making it easier to analyze the data.
- **Zoom**: This button opens a dialog box that allows you to set a specific zoom level (e.g., 75%, 100%, 200%).
- **100%**: Returns the zoom level to 100%, showing the worksheet in the standard size.
- **Fit Selection**: Automatically resizes the zoom level to fit the selected range of cells in the window, which helps view a whole dataset.

Window

The **Window** section allows you to manage multiple work windows simultaneously, making it easy to compare worksheets or different sections of the same sheet.
- **New Window**: This opens a new window of the current document, allowing you to view and work on different parts of the same file simultaneously.
- **Arrange All**: Automatically arrange all open windows on the screen, tiling them horizontally or vertically to facilitate comparing spreadsheets.
- **View Side by Side**: This option allows you to view two worksheets side by side, which is useful for quickly comparing data or file versions.
- **Synchronous scrolling**: When viewing two worksheets side by side, this feature synchronizes scrolling, allowing you to scroll through data simultaneously in both windows.
- **Reset Window Position**: Returns side-by-side windows to their original position after resizing or moving them.
- **Change Window**: This feature allows you to quickly switch between all open Excel windows, making it easier to manage multiple files.

Macros

The **Macros** section is dedicated to automating repetitive or complex processes using macros, which can be recorded and repeated automatically.
- **View Macros**: This option shows all macros created or available in the worksheet, allowing you to run, edit, or delete existing macros.
- **Record Macros**: Record a sequence of operations performed in the worksheet to automate and repeat them with a single click. Macros are handy for repetitive tasks involving complex data.
- **Use macros**: This option allows you to run a previously recorded or created macro, automating operations with a simple click.

Excel macros are potent tools that simplify your work, especially when dealing with repetitive and tedious tasks. Suppose you've ever felt overwhelmed by the number of manual operations you must perform or are concerned about making mistakes while entering data or formatting large amounts of information. In that case, macros are the solution you need. Macros allow you to automate these actions, saving time and minimizing errors. Imagine formatting a group of cells in a specific way or applying a set of calculations to different data groups. A macro lets you record these operations once, and then, with just one click, you can repeat those same operations whenever you need to. This saves you the hassle of doing everything manually and ensures that the tasks are done consistently, reducing the risk of mistakes caused by distractions or haste.

Using macros might feel intimidating, especially if you know that learning to automate tasks could be complicated. But the good news is that you don't need to be a programming expert to start using macros in Excel. Thanks to Excel's recording feature, you can create macros by recording your actions in the spreadsheet. This means you can make a macro without touching a single line of code. Once recorded, the macro can be triggered whenever needed, helping you speed up your workflow and feel more confident in tasks you repeat often.

Excel macros allow you to work more efficiently by eliminating the need to manually repeat the same operations, and they help you manage your time better. With macros, you'll be more productive and at ease, knowing that Excel handles the details, allowing you to focus on more important decisions. So, suppose tackling repetitive and tedious tasks worries you, or you're afraid of making mistakes during critical stages of your work. In that case, macros can transform your work experience by bringing order and precision while giving you the peace of mind that you're saving valuable time.

5. Microsoft PowerPoint 2025

Microsoft PowerPoint 2025 is an indispensable tool for visually appealing and professionally effective presentations. In business, academic, and creative environments, PowerPoint allows you to organize and present ideas, projects and reports engagingly. With new features and improvements, PowerPoint 2025 makes creating dynamic and interactive presentations easier, allowing you to customize every aspect of the design, from slides to transitions. In this chapter, we'll look at the essential features of PowerPoint, from the initial layout to the creation of multimedia content to advanced techniques to improve the quality of your presentations.

Microsoft PowerPoint 2025 represents the latest evolution of one of the most versatile and widely used tools for creating digital presentations. Whether you're working on a business, academic, or creative project, PowerPoint provides an intuitive and powerful platform to **organize ideas**, **share information,** and **communicate messages visually** and effectively. Its popularity stems from its ease of use combined with a comprehensive range of features that allow you to create engaging presentations, whether for live presentations or online content.

Essential features for presentations

PowerPoint 2025 offers several **essential features** that allow you to professionally bring your ideas to life. These include the possibility of:

- **Create custom slides**: With PowerPoint, you can easily add slides, choose specific layouts, and customize every graphic appearance. PowerPoint's flexibility allows you to design presentations tailored to your audience's needs, using text, images, charts, videos, and interactive multimedia content.
- **Organize information**: With pre-built templates and formatting options, you can organize your content clearly and readably, improving your understanding of your message. PowerPoint 2025 also introduces smart suggestions to optimize the layout based on the data type you're entering.
- **Collaboration and sharing**: Integration with **Microsoft 365** and **OneDrive** allows for real-time collaboration, allowing multiple people to simultaneously work on the same presentation. This is especially useful when working on group projects or with teams across different locations.

PowerPoint 2025 continues to improve presentation management, introducing new features that make it easier to organize slides and use interactive elements. These features make PowerPoint ideal for traditional presentations and more dynamic visual content like tutorials, lectures, or business pitches.

How to get and use PowerPoint for free

Suppose you want to use PowerPoint but need help accessing the full version through a **Microsoft Office 365 subscription**. In that case, there are free options that still allow you to take advantage of most of its features:

- **PowerPoint Online**: Microsoft offers a free version of PowerPoint that can be accessed directly from the browser, known as PowerPoint Online. While slightly limited compared to the desktop

version, this allows you to create and edit presentations, share them, and collaborate with others in real-time. Just create a Microsoft account and sign in via the **Office.com site**.
- **PowerPoint Mobile**: If you prefer to work on the go, PowerPoint is also available as a mobile app (Android and iOS). This version is free for devices with small screen sizes and allows you to view, edit, and create presentations from your smartphone or tablet.

Free access to PowerPoint offers an excellent solution for those needing presentation software without necessarily purchasing a full Office subscription. While some advanced features may not be available online or mobile, these options still allow you to produce high-quality presentations.

Home

The **PowerPoint Home** tab contains all the main tools for creating, formatting, and organizing the slides in a presentation. It offers quick access to basic features such as **copy/paste**, slide management, text formatting, and graphic insertion. In addition, this tab includes advanced tools to collaborate with other users in real-time, add comments, and even record the presentation, even with external cameras such as those on the phone.

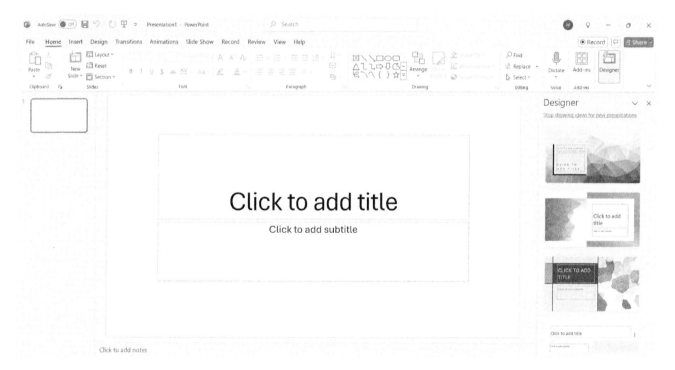

Paste

This button lets you paste content copied to the clipboard, such as text, images, charts, or shapes, directly onto the slide. It also includes a drop-down menu with several paste options:
- **Keep Original Formatting**: Paste the content while maintaining the style and formatting of the copied item.
- **Paste as Plain Text**: This option pastes text without formatting, which is useful when you want to integrate text into your existing layout.

71

- **Paste as Image**: Converts the copied content into an image.

Slides

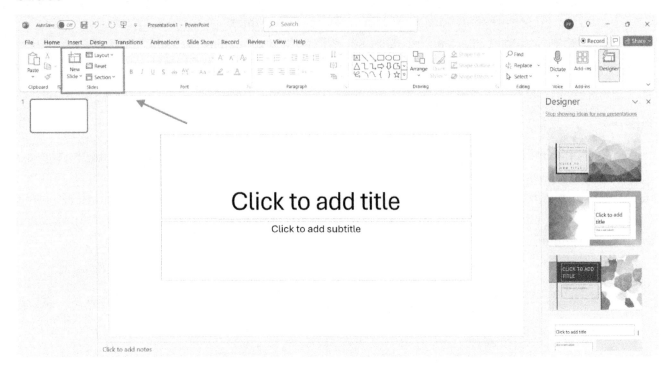

- **New Slide**: This option adds a new slide to your presentation, and you can choose from various predefined layouts, such as "Title & Content," "Two Content," "Title Only," and many more.
- **Layout**: Changes the design of the selected slide, allowing you to choose from different content structures such as text only, media, charts, or tables.
- **Section**: Organize your presentation into sections. Sections are especially useful for long presentations because they allow you to group related slides logically and orderly.
- **Revert** Returns a slide to its original layout, eliminating unwanted structural changes.

Text formatting

This section is crucial for managing and customizing text within slides. You can change the style, size, and color of the text, enhancing the aesthetics of your presentation.
- **Font**: Change the font of the selected text. You can choose from the fonts available in the system or theme fonts.
- **Font size**: Increase or decrease the size of the selected text to better fit the slide layout.
- **Bold, Italic, Underline**: These options allow you to emphasize parts of the text with different styles.
- **Text Color**: You can change the color of the text by choosing theme colors or customizing a specific color.
- **Text alignment**: Adjust text alignment (left, center, correct, or justified) to improve the readability and aesthetics of your presentation.

- **Bulleted and numbered lists**: Organize text into bulleted lists, making creating critical points or structured lists easy.
- **Line spacing**: This allows you to adjust the spacing between lines of text, making the content more readable.

Inserting Images and Shapes

This section enriches your presentation with visual elements such as images, shapes, and text boxes.

- **Images**: This option allows you to insert images from your computer or online sources. The image can be resized, rotated, and moved freely within the slide.
- **Shapes**: This feature inserts predefined shapes such as rectangles, arrows, ovals, lines, and many more. Shapes can be customized in terms of color, outline, and size.
- **Text Box**: This option inserts an independent text box on the slide, which is useful for adding custom titles or descriptions.
- **Convert to SmartArt Graphic**: This function turns a list of text into a SmartArt chart, which is useful for displaying text in the form of diagrams, processes, hierarchies, or loops.

1. Add-ons

- **Add-ins**: Provides access to external tools integrated with PowerPoint to extend functionality. You can install add-ons from the **Microsoft Store** or other sources. These tools can be helpful for advanced analytics, interactive content creation, or integrations with different platforms.

Share with OneDrive

PowerPoint, integrated with **OneDrive**, makes it easy to save and share files with others and collaborate in real-time.

- **Share**: Upload your presentation to **OneDrive** and share it with others. With OneDrive, you can invite collaborators to view or edit your presentation in real time. Collaborators can access the presentation from any connected device, which makes it easy to work together on important presentations.
- **Permission management**: While sharing, you can set access levels (view or edit) and control who has access to the presentation.

Remarks

- **Comments**: This feature allows you to add comments on any presentation element, making it easier to review collaboratively. Comments can be linked to specific objects or text on the slide, allowing you to receive feedback or suggestions on changes needed.
  - **Reply to comments**: Comments allow for in-threaded conversations, so multiple users can discuss a change directly within the file.
  - **Comment Navigation**: Allows you to quickly switch between comments, making it easy to thoroughly review your presentation.

Record

- **Record Screen**: This feature allows you to record the content of your screen, which helps create tutorials or video presentations. You can record a demonstration of your work or add narrations to explain the contents of your presentation.
- **Video recording with phone camera**: In addition to screen recording, you can now connect your phone's cameras to record videos directly in PowerPoint. This feature allows you to add personal video presentations, where the user can be seen while explaining the slide.
- **Record Presentation**: This will enable you to record your entire presentation with audio or video narration, including slide content and animations or transitions. Ideal for creating presentations to distribute as video files or for online meetings.

Enter

The Insert tab in PowerPoint is one of the most important, as it allows you to enrich your presentation with a wide range of graphic and multimedia elements. In addition to slide management, the **Insert** tab will enable you to add tables, images, charts, links, text boxes, videos, and more, turning a simple slide sequence into a dynamic and interactive presentation.

Slides

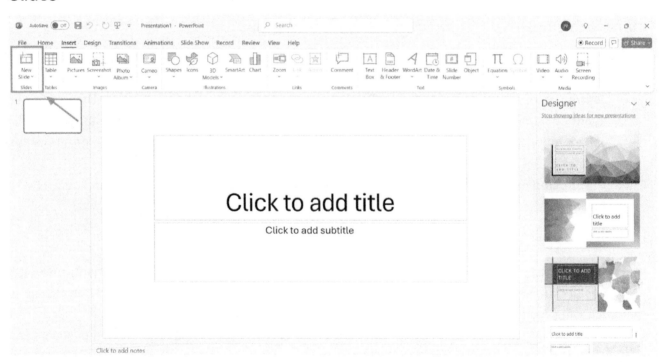

New Slide: This option allows you to add a new slide to your presentation. You can choose from predefined layouts such as "Title & Content," "Two Content," "Title Only," and others specific to various types of content.

Tables

This option inserts a table directly into the slide. You can choose the number of rows and columns when you insert them and then customize the table with advanced formatting such as colors, borders, and styles. Tables are useful for organizing and displaying data clearly and structured.

Images

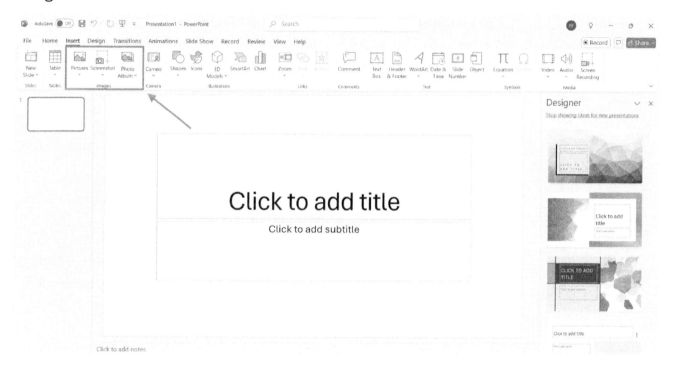

- **Image from File**: This option allows you to insert images saved on your computer. You can resize, move, and format these images directly on the slide.
- **Online images**: It allows you to search for and insert pictures from online sources, such as **Bing** or **OneDrive**, making it easy to insert creative photos without leaving PowerPoint.
- **Screenshot**: This function captures the image of the screen or an active window on your computer and inserts it directly into the slide. It is useful for inserting application screens or windows for demonstrations and tutorials.

Shapes

This feature allows you to insert predefined geometric shapes such as rectangles, circles, arrows, lines, and other customizable shapes. Once inserted, shapes can be modified in color, fill, outline, and special effects. Shapes are useful for creating custom charts, diagrams, and illustrations directly within your slides.

Icons

This function inserts predefined icons from a large built-in library of vector icons. Icons can be resized without loss of quality and are ideal for representing visual concepts or enriching the slide layout with simple but effective graphic elements.

3D Models

3D models: Allows you to insert three-dimensional models directly into the slide. The 3D models can be rotated and viewed from different angles, making the presentation more interactive and visually appealing. PowerPoint offers a library of 3D models or allows you to upload custom models.

Charts

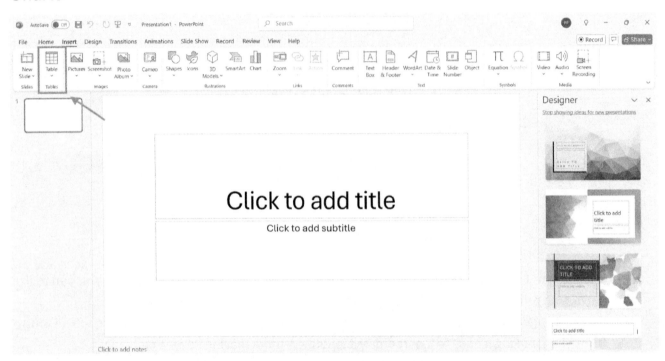

Insert a chart into the slide, such as a column, bar, line, pie chart, etc. Charts are linked to a built-in Excel table, allowing you to insert and edit data directly within PowerPoint. They help display statistical data, comparisons, or trends clearly and professionally.

Links

- **Hyperlink**: Create a link to a web page, another slide in your presentation, an external file, or an email address. Hyperlinks help create an interactive presentation, allowing viewers to navigate different content.
- **Bookmark**: Insert a bookmark on a slide to facilitate internal navigation. You can create links to specific presentation sections with bookmarks, improving organization and navigability.

Text boxes

- **Text Box**: This option inserts an independent text box within the slide. The text box can be moved and resized freely and is useful for adding titles, subtitles, or custom text blocks. Text boxes can also be formatted in various ways, such as changing the color, alignment, or line spacing.

WordArt

- **WordArt** adds decorative text with special effects, such as shading, outlines, skewing, and rotation. It is useful for creating headings or sections that grab attention with an eye-catching, personalized visual style.

Slide Numbers

Slide Number: This feature adds numbers to the slides in your presentation. It is especially useful in long or structured presentations, where it is important to keep track of the number of slides. The slide number can be placed in headers, footers, or other custom locations.

Equations and Symbols

- **Equation**: This tool allows you to enter predefined or custom mathematical equations. The equation editor supports a wide range of mathematical symbols and operations, making it ideal for technical or academic presentations that require complex mathematical expressions.
- **Symbols**: Inserts special symbols, such as monetary characters, accented letters, or mathematical symbols. You can choose from an extensive library of symbols, which are helpful when using characters not generally found on your keyboard.

Video

- **Video from File**: This option inserts a video file directly into the slide. The video can be resized, trimmed, and customized with playback effects. You can use videos saved on your computer or insert videos from online sources like YouTube.
- **Online Video**: This feature allows you to link and embed a video from an online platform, such as **YouTube**, directly within the slide. It is useful for including multimedia content without having to download or import it locally.
- **Video tools**: Once you've inserted a video, PowerPoint offers tools to change playback, add transitions and animations, or even hide video controls for a smoother presentation experience.

Audio

- **Audio from file**: You can insert an audio file directly into the slide, such as a music track or voice commentary. The audio file can be played automatically or manually controlled during the presentation.
- **Audio Recording**: This feature allows you to record a voice narration directly in PowerPoint and insert it into the slide. It is useful for presentations that require narration or voice explanations.
- **Audio tools**: Once you've inserted an audio file, PowerPoint offers tools to customize its playback, such as setting the volume, duration, and how to start (automatic or manual).

Drawing

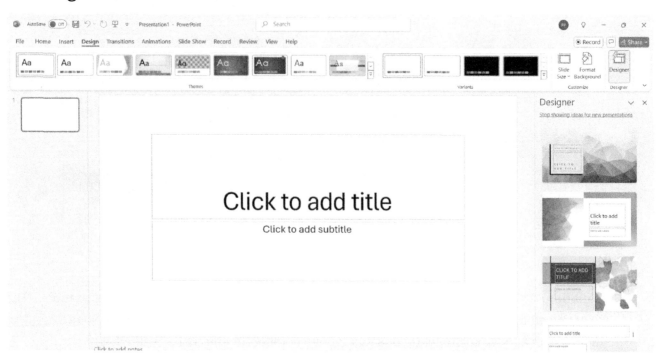

The **Drawing** tab in PowerPoint is primarily designed for touch devices, such as tablets and iPads, where you can interact directly with the screen using a digital pen or your fingers. This tab allows you to draw freehand, annotate slides, and create visual content quickly and intuitively. It's beneficial for mobile workers who need to make quick edits or add custom annotations to slides without using a keyboard.

Design

Pen: The primary tool for freehand drawing on slides. You can choose from different types of pens (such as fountain pens, markers, and pencils) and customize the stroke in terms of thickness and color. Pens allow you to draw directly on slides to add annotations, diagrams, or simple illustrations.

- **Colors and thicknesses**: PowerPoint allows you to choose from a wide range of colors for strokes and adjust the thickness of the pen to achieve different visual results.
- **Highlighter**: Besides pens, you can use a highlighter to highlight parts of the text or specific areas of the slide with transparent colors.

Eraser

Tool used to erase manually drawn strokes. Different sizes of rubber are available:

- **Small eraser**: Ideal for accurately erasing small areas of the design or specific details.
- **Medium and Large Eraser**: This tool quickly erases larger areas, which is useful when deleting entire strokes or sections of the drawing.
- **Stroke Eraser**: This option lets you remove entire drawing strokes in one step without manually erasing every small part.

Lasso selection

Useful tool for selecting specific parts of your freehand drawing. With lasso selection, you can surround drawn elements to select them and then edit, move, or delete them. This tool is handy when working with hand-drawn strokes that can't be chosen as text elements or standard shapes.

Pen Types

PowerPoint offers a variety of writing/drawing tools, each with a different visual effect. These tools are handy for simulating different writing styles, such as formal or artistic writing.

- **Ballpoint pen**: A standard-style pen suitable for taking notes or annotating with a delicate and precise stroke.
- **Fountain pen**: This simulates a fountain pen with thicker and more flexible strokes, which is ideal for creating signatures or more elaborate designs.
- **Pencil**: Reproduces the effect of a pencil, which is helpful for freehand drawings or quick sketches.
- **Marker**: Creates thicker, bolder strokes, suitable for highlighting or drawing significant elements.
- **Highlighter**: Highlights parts of the text or slide with semi-transparent colors.

Ink to Text

- **Convert to Text**: One of the most advanced features of the Drawing tab is the ability to convert handwritten text into plain text. After writing freehand on a slide, PowerPoint uses a handwriting recognition system to turn the drawn text into digital, editable text. This tool is handy when taking notes quickly and converting them into professionally formatted text.

Inserting Shapes and Equations

- **Convert drawing to shapes**: PowerPoint allows you to transform freehand drawings into perfect geometric shapes. For example, if you draw a circle or square by hand, the **Convert to Shapes feature** will turn it into a smooth, clean geometric shape. This is useful for creating diagrams or schematics without using predefined shapes.
- **Equations**: You can draw freehand equations, and PowerPoint automatically converts them into formatted equations. This is especially useful for scientific or mathematical presentations, where complex equations must be written clearly and legibly.

Design

The **Design** tab in PowerPoint is essential for creating presentations that look great and professional without having advanced graphic design skills. This tab allows you to apply predefined and custom styles, adjust the slide size, and manage the overall look and feel of the slides. In addition, it offers tools such as **Designer**, an AI-powered service that suggests visual layouts based on the contents of the presentation. While this AI feature is still evolving, Microsoft is working to improve it. It will offer an increasingly intuitive and robust experience.

Themes

- **Default themes**: PowerPoint provides a wide range of **predefined themes**, which offer comprehensive visual styles for your presentation, including color schemes, fonts, and layouts. These themes can be applied with a single click and instantly give all slides a uniform and professional look.
    - Each theme includes several pre-made layouts that help maintain graphical consistency in the arrangement of elements such as titles, content, and images.
- **Theme customization**: PowerPoint allows customization by changing colors, fonts, and associated effects. You can create a theme unique to your brand or project and save it for future use, ensuring that all presentations have a visually consistent look.
- **Custom themes**: Once you've created a custom theme, you can save it for other presentations or share it with others. This feature is especially useful in businesses, where all presentations must follow a brand's guidelines.

Variants

- **Variations**: Each default theme offers **variations**, which allow you to apply minor stylistic changes, such as color or font changes while maintaining the overall graphic scheme. Variations allow you to give a unique and personalized look without distorting the basic theme.
1. Slide Size

- **Slide size**: This tool allows you to choose the size of the slides, both in **16:9** aspect ratio (widescreen screen, standard for presentations on modern screens) and **4:3** (standard for projectors or older screens). PowerPoint also offers the ability to customize the size, which is useful when working with specific formats for printing or other applications.

Background

- **Background formatting**: PowerPoint allows you to customize the background of your slides to add color, images, or texture. You can apply a background to a single slide or all slides in your presentation.
    - **Background Color**: Choose a solid color as the background of the slide.
    - **Image or Texture Background**: This feature allows you to insert an image or texture as a background. It is useful when you want to make a stronger visual impact or use a custom background, such as your company logo.
    - **Background transparency**: PowerPoint offers the ability to adjust the transparency of the background, which helps keep the focus on overlapping elements while maintaining a visual touch in the background.

Designer

This feature leverages artificial intelligence to help you create professional-looking slides. When you insert content, such as images or text, **the Designer** automatically analyzes the layout and suggests optimized designs to enhance the presentation.

- **Real-time suggestions**: The designer offers eye-catching visual layouts based on the content you've entered. For example, if you add an image, the Designer will suggest how to align and arrange it in the most effective way with respect to the text.
- **Automatic customization**: As you add new elements, the Designer continuously updates its proposals, offering design ideas to keep the presentation modern and visually pleasing.

Note: Although Designer is currently under development and improvement, Microsoft is investing heavily in this feature and plans to expand its capabilities, making the design process more accessible and more automated.

Graphic effects

The Design tab allows you to add **visual effects** that apply to various slide elements. These effects, such as shadows, reflections, glows, and angles, enhance the aesthetic appearance of graphics, images, and text within your slides, making your presentation more dynamic and appealing.

Transitions

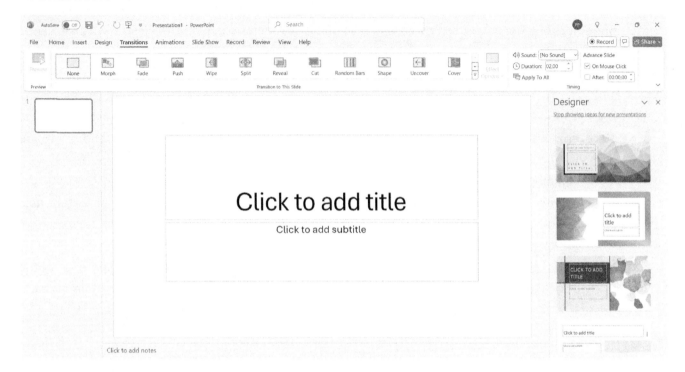

The **Transitions** tab in PowerPoint provides tools to manage animations between slides, improving the flow of your presentation and keeping your audience's attention. Transitions are essential for determining how slides change, adding an element of dynamism to your presentation. However, choosing the type of transition is necessary based on the audience and context. Some more elaborate transitions may be inappropriate in formal settings, while in more creative or informal presentations, they can add an interesting visual touch.

Preview Transitions

Whenever you select a transition, PowerPoint shows you an instant preview of what it will look like. This feature is helpful for quickly viewing the chosen effect without starting the entire slideshow. The preview helps you determine if a transition is appropriate for the style and tone of your presentation.

Selecting transitions

The transitions window features **predefined animations** to apply to your slides. These transitions are divided into three categories:

- **Slim**: Simple, professional effects, such as "Fade" or "Cut," ideal for business or academic presentations.
- **Dynamic**: These are more elaborate and visually appealing transitions, such as "Move" or "Morph," suitable for more creative presentations.

82

- **Eye-catching**: More complex and creative transitions, such as "Cube" or "Page turn," that can capture your audience's attention. These transitions are ideal for less formal presentations or younger audiences.

Each transition has a different visual impact, and choosing the right one depends on the tone of the presentation and the type of audience. For example, a more sober transition suits a formal business presentation, while a more dynamic one can be used in a more creative or educational context.

Effect Options

Each transition can be customized further using the effect options. For example, with the "Push" transition, you can choose the direction from which the next slide comes (from left, right, up, or down). These options allow you to tailor the transition to the specific needs of your presentation, giving you more control over the aesthetics of the transition from one slide to another.

Duration

The Duration button allows you to adjust the time it takes to complete the transition between slides. Increasing the duration slows the transition while reducing it speeds it up. This control is important for managing the pace of your presentation and maintaining a consistent flow.
- **Tip**: Short transitions (0.5-1 second) can be effective for a more dynamic and faster presentation. Longer durations can enhance the visual effect in a more relaxed environment or emphasize a transition.

Audio

PowerPoint also allows you to add **sound effects** to your transitions. You can select a predefined sound (such as "Doorbell," "Applause," or "Scroll") or upload a custom audio file. Audio can capture your audience's attention during a critical transition. Still, it should be used sparingly to avoid distracting attention from the main content of your presentation.

Slide Progress

PowerPoint offers two ways to advance slides during your presentation:
- **On Mouse Click**: This setting allows you to manually advance to the next slide by clicking the mouse. It's useful when you want total control over your presentation's pace, deciding when to move to the next slide based on context or audience.
- **After a time interval**: Alternatively, you can set a specific time, after which the slide will automatically move to the next. This option is handy for automatic presentations or "loop" mode, such as presentations for trade fairs or information kiosks, where slides advance without user intervention.

Tip: When using the auto-advance option, it's important to synchronize the transition time with the duration needed to discuss the slide's contents. If the time is too short, you risk passing too quickly; if it's too long, your audience may lose interest.

Animations

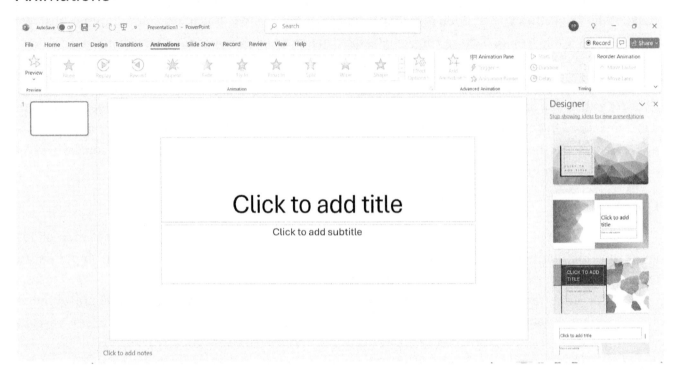

The **Animations** tab is one of PowerPoint's most creative and powerful tools, capable of transforming a static presentation into a visually engaging experience. Animations help capture your audience's attention and allow you to emphasize key points, control the flow of information, and create a smoother, more dynamic narrative. In this tab, you can choose from various animations for objects on your slides, such as text, images, shapes, and charts, and customize them in detail to achieve the desired effect.

Types of animations

Animations in PowerPoint are divided into several main categories, each of which has a specific purpose to enhance the interactivity of the presentation:
- **Entrance Animations**: These animations determine how an object (text, image, chart, etc.) appears on the slide. Entrance effects are helpful in sequentially introducing new elements, allowing the presenter to focus on one point at a time. Some examples include:
    - **Appearance**: The object appears quickly and discreetly.
    - **Fade In**: The object appears gradually, fading into the slide.
    - **Twirl:** The object rotates or twirls as it appears.
- **Emphasis animations**: These animations highlight an object already on the slide, keeping the audience's attention on a specific point. Some common effects include:
    - **Fill Color**: Temporarily changes the color of an object to make it stand out.

- **Swing**: Swings the object to attract attention.
  - **Pulsation**: The object expands and contracts to give the idea of continuous motion.
- **Exit Animations**: These animations determine how an object disappears from the slide. They are ideal for summarizing a topic before moving on to a new concept or point. Some examples of exit effects include:
  - **Fade**: The object slowly fades out until it disappears.
  - **Bounce Out**: The object "bounces" as it leaves the slide.
  - **Scroll Out**: The object slides off the slide in a specified direction (left, right, up, down).
- **Motion paths**: These custom animations allow you to have objects follow a predefined or manually drawn path on the slide. For example, you can make an icon "fly" from one side of the slide to the other or have an image follow a curved path.
  - **Custom Path**: Manually draw the path the object will follow on the slide.
  - **Lines, curves, and arcs** Allow you to set predefined paths for the movement of the object, which helps give images or shapes a realistic sense of movement.

Effect Options

Each animation can be further customized through effect **options**, which allow you to choose which direction an object enters or exits the slide, the speed of movement, and other specific parameters.

- **Direction**: Sets which side of the slide the object should enter or exit. For example, a text can "scroll" from the left, right, up, or down.
- **Speed**: You can adjust the time in seconds to choose how fast or slow an animation should be completed. This allows you to adapt the animation to the pace of the presentation.
- **Sequence**: Some text animations allow you to decide whether to animate all the text simultaneously, individual words, or even individual characters, adding a progressive reveal effect.

Animation Pane

The **Animation Pane** is an essential tool for a complete and detailed overview of the animations applied to the objects on the slide. This panel allows you to manage the order of the animations, change their duration, and set the time relationships between them.

- **Change the order**: You can reorder animations by dragging them in the animation pane to appear in the correct sequence.
- **Timing setting**: You can set animations to start automatically with the slide or by clicking the mouse. This allows you to control the presentation flow according to your needs.
- **Duration and Delay**: Adjust the duration of each animation and set a delay between the start of the transition and the animation. This allows you to perfectly synchronize the animation with the rhythm of your presentation or speeches.

Advanced Animation

- **Start by clicking with the previous one and after the previous** one. These timing options allow you to decide when to start the animation compared to the others. You can start an animation with the mouse click at the same time as another build (with the previous one) or after another build has been completed (after the previous one). This gives you detailed control over the sequence of animations.

Preview

When you apply an animation, you can preview the result directly on the current slide. This feature lets you immediately test the visual effect and check if it aligns with your expectations. You can also play the entire sequence of animations on a slide to control the total flow.

Duration

The Duration button allows you to adjust the length of an animation. This allows you to adapt the animation's speed to the presentation's pace. For example, a fade effect can last a few seconds or be slowed down to create more visual impact.

Customizing and enhancing animations

One of the best features of the **Animations** tab is the ability **to test, enhance, and customize** animations as needed by your presentation. Once you've applied an animation, you can:

- **See the effect on the individual slide**: With the preview, you can control how the animations look on the specific slide. This allows you to experiment with different combinations of effects until you get the desired result.
- **Edit and enhance animations**: If the visual impact doesn't match your expectations, you can quickly go back and enhance or replace the animation with another. Combining entrance, emphasis, exit, and path animations allows creative flexibility.

Slide Show

The PowerPoint **Slide Show** tab is the starting point for checking how your presentation will appear to your audience. Once you've prepared all your slides, set up your animations, and choose your layouts, this tab lets you start and check your actual presentation. Here, you can manage how your slides will be presented, choosing from various modes such as presenter or custom view. You can also adjust intervals, audio, and subtitles, making the experience smoother for the presenter and the audience.

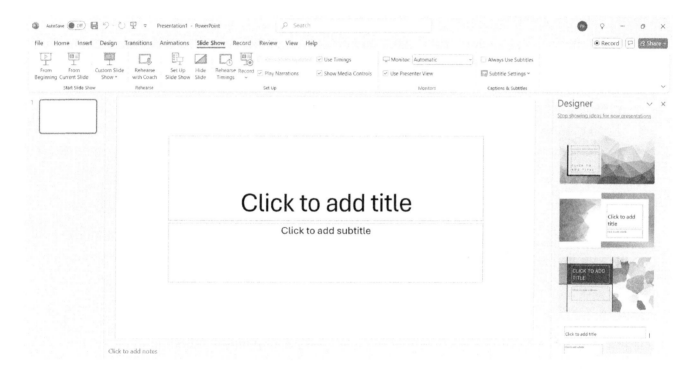

Start Slide Show

This section allows you to start the presentation in different ways:
- **From the beginning**: Start the presentation from the first slide, showing it in full-screen mode. This is the standard option for checking the overall look of your presentation and conducting a dress rehearsal.
- **From Current Slide**: This option allows you to start the presentation from the selected slide without returning to the beginning. It helps review specific presentation sections without scrolling through all the slides.
- **Custom Presentation**: This option allows you to create a custom sequence of slides, which is useful when you want to show only certain parts of your presentation to a specific audience. With this option, you can configure different versions of your presentation, each with a custom order of the slides.

Presenter View

Presenter view allows you to see your presentation on two screens: the audience sees the slide in full screen, while the presenter sees an interface with additional functionality. This interface includes a preview of subsequent slides, speaker notes, and a timer to keep track of the presentation time. This mode is perfect for presenters who want more control during their presentations. It allows you to avoid surprises with subsequent slides.

Set Up Presentation

- **Full-screen presentation**: This is the standard option for in-person or virtual presentations, and it shows the presentation in full screen without toolbars or distractions.
- **Slideshow in a window**: Shows the slideshow in a resizable window, which is helpful for presentations in web conferences or when you need to keep other windows open.
- **Repeat Until Interrupted (Loop)**: This feature sets the slideshow to automatically repeat when it is complete until it is interrupted. It is useful for presentations displayed in a loop, such as those at trade shows or reception areas.

Hide Slide

- **Hide Slide**: This feature temporarily excludes a slide from the slide show sequence. The slide will not be shown during the presentation but will remain in the file. This feature is useful when you want to flexibly adapt your presentation for different audiences without deleting the content.

Intervals

Timing management allows you to determine how long each slide is displayed and how long it can be transitioned. This feature is handy for automated presentations.

- **Test Timings**: This option allows you to rehearse the presentation while setting the duration intervals for each slide. During this mode, PowerPoint records how much time you spend on each slide and automatically applies those intervals, making it possible to play the presentation without the need for a presenter to click between slides.
- **Use Recorded** Ranges: Once you have recorded the ranges, you can use them. If you disable this option, you must manually advance through the slides.

Audio narration and intervals

- **Record Presentation**: This feature lets you record your voice commenting on the slides. You can choose whether to record audio narration only or include intervals. Recording can be helpful for presentations that will be distributed as video files or used in environments where the presenter is not physically present.
- **Include narration and intervals**: When you activate this option, PowerPoint will play the recorded audio and intervals of the presentation, making it fully automated. It helps create a self-contained presentation where the audience can listen to the narration without the speaker's intervention.

Audio

- **Audio settings**: During your presentation, you can include audio files or background music that start automatically when you switch to specific slides. You can also control the volume and decide whether the audio should play automatically or with a mouse click. Pre-recorded audio is beneficial in contexts with no live speaker, such as presentations at trade shows or information points.

Subtitles

- **Enable Subtitles**: PowerPoint allows you to turn on **subtitles** during your presentation. This feature is handy in multilingual presentations or when there are people with hearing disabilities in the audience. Subtitles can be generated in real-time using your voice or preset with a text file.
- **Subtitle Settings**: Allows you to customize the subtitle language, their position, and style. For example, you can display subtitles at the top or bottom of the slide and adjust the text format.

Monitor

- **Set up monitors**: If you're using multiple monitors, this option allows you to configure which monitor PowerPoint will use to show your presentation. You can show your slides to your audience on one screen while holding the presenter's view on another.

Records

The **Record** tab in PowerPoint is one of the most powerful features for creating interactive and multimedia presentations. With this tab, you can record your entire presentation, including narration, intervals, annotations, and animations, and later export it as a **video file**. This tool is handy for creating educational content, tutorials, or presentations that must be distributed online or shared with audiences who can't attend live.

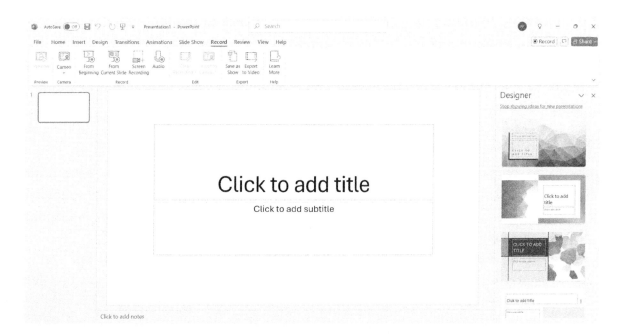

Record Presentation

The primary function of **the Record tab** is the ability to record your presentation in real time, including narration, webcam video, and annotations on the slide.

- **Record from Beginning**: This option allows you to start recording your presentation from the **first slide**. Everything said and shown will be recorded, including animation movements, voice narration, and videos. It is ideal for recording a complete slideshow that can be played back as a video file.
- **Record from Current Slide**: If you have already recorded part of the presentation or want to record a specific section, this option allows you to start recording from the **selected slide**. This is useful when you want to record only certain parts or if you need to update the recording of a specific slide without redoing the entire presentation.
- **Recording options**: During recording, you can include only audio narration, video (if using a webcam), and/or annotations made with pens and highlighters. This gives you total control over what to record and how to customize the slideshow.

Export your slideshow as a video.

Once the recording is complete, PowerPoint allows you to **export the presentation as a video file**. This is useful for creating content that can be viewed independently of the speaker, shared online, or included on platforms like YouTube or Vimeo.

- **Video formats**: PowerPoint allows you to export your presentation to various formats, including **MP4** or **WMV**. The MP4 format is generally preferable since it is compatible with most devices and platforms.
- **Video Quality**: You can choose from several video quality options, such as:
  - **Ultra HD (4K) quality**: For the highest quality video, suitable for large screens or projectors.
  - **Full HD (1080p) quality**: Ideal for most video presentations in professional settings.
  - **HD Quality (720p):** Suitable for sharing content online or via email.
  - **Standard Quality**: Useful when it is essential to reduce the file size.
- **Include Intervals and Narrations**: When you export the video file, PowerPoint allows you to include **the recorded intervals** and **narrations**. This is essential if you've added audio narration or set specific transition times between slides.

Personalization of the recording

In addition to the entire recording, PowerPoint allows you to customize your recording in several ways:

- **Selecting Slides to Record**: You can record the entire presentation or just a few **specific slides**. For example, you only need to edit or add content to a part of the presentation. In that case, you can record those slides exclusively.
- **Incremental recording**: You can record your presentation in multiple batches, starting and stopping the recording at different times. This allows you to correct errors or update only certain presentation sections.

Audio and Video Options

- **Audio narration**: You can record narration for the duration of the presentation using your computer's built-in microphone or an external microphone. This option allows you to explain and comment on each slide as it is displayed.
- **Webcam Video Recording**: To add a more personal touch to your presentation, you can also include a **video** of yourself using your webcam. Video recording can make your presentation more engaging, especially in educational or training settings.
- **Freehand annotations**: While recording, you can also use digital pens or highlighting tools to add **freehand annotations** to your slides. This is useful for explaining complex concepts or underlining key points while speaking.

Playback of the recording

Once the recording is complete, you can play it directly within PowerPoint to verify that everything has been recorded correctly and that the narrations and intervals are in sync. If necessary, you can go back and **edit or re-record** specific parts of your presentation.

1. Recorded Presentation Settings
- **Intervals**: When you export the slideshow as a video, you can choose whether to include recorded intervals. Intervals determine how long each slide is displayed before proceeding to the next.
- **Separate audio and video**: You can include only audio or video in the recording, excluding the other elements. This flexibility allows you to customize your presentation for different scenarios, such as removing narration for an audience that doesn't need it.

Re-Register

Suppose the first recording does not meet your expectations, or you want to correct any errors. In that case, you can easily repeat the recording of a single slide or the entire presentation. This tool allows you to continuously refine your presentation until you get the desired result.

Revision

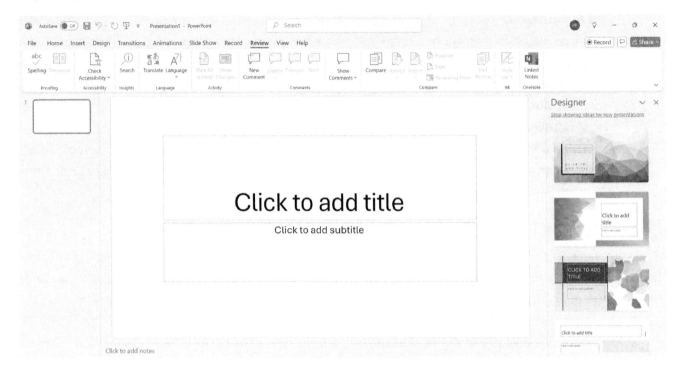

The **Review** tab in PowerPoint provides tools to help you review and proofread your text, as well as translation and collaboration capabilities. Even though PowerPoint tends to use less text than Word, it's essential to ensure that every text element is correct, especially in professional presentations. The Review tab provides Word-like tools for correcting typos, checking grammar, translating content, and managing comments. However, PowerPoint's focus is often more visual, emphasizing images and charts rather than long blocks of text.

Spell check

An essential tool that checks text spelling on your slides. Even though PowerPoint presentations often include less text than Word documents, ensuring the text is error-free is still crucial. PowerPoint highlights words with errors and suggests corrections. You can add words to the dictionary if they are technical terms or proper nouns.

- **Proofreading suggestions**: PowerPoint provides automatic suggestions to correct typos or spelling mistakes.
- **Ignore**: Allows you to ignore an error for a given word if it is deemed correct in that context.
- **Add to the dictionary**: For unrecognized words that are correct, you can add them to the dictionary to prevent them from being flagged as errors in the future.

Translation

The translation feature allows you to directly translate selected text from one language to another within PowerPoint. This is useful when you need to present the same content to a multilingual audience or when you need to translate individual terms or phrases.

- **Language selection**: PowerPoint allows you to choose from various languages. You can translate a word, a sentence, or an entire text box, and the translation will be automatically inserted into the slide.
- **Online translation service**: PowerPoint connects with an online translation service to get instant and accurate translations. This feature may require an active internet connection.

Remarks

New Comment allows you to add **comments** to your slides, which is useful for multi-person collaborations and reviews. Although PowerPoint doesn't have as large blocks of text as Word, comments allow you to jot down ideas, suggestions, or revisions for images, charts, or other visual elements in your presentation.

- **Reply to comments**: PowerPoint allows you to create discussion threads where various collaborators can reply to previous comments and discuss changes to be made.
- **Comment navigation**: With navigation buttons, you can easily switch between comments to review and reply to notes left by collaborators.
- **Delete Comment**: Once a comment has been resolved or is no longer relevant, you can delete it to keep the presentation clean and organized.

Intelligent Search (Search Insights)

This feature lets you get additional information about a term or phrase directly from the slide. It links to online search services and provides details, definitions, or even images related to the term you seek. This tool helps delve deeper into content without leaving PowerPoint.

- **Internet search**: When you select a word or phrase, PowerPoint performs a web search and shows you results, such as definitions, articles, or other resources.

Language

You can set the spelling and grammar-checking language for specific text sections. This is useful when working with multilingual presentations or technical terms that belong to different languages. For example, you can set one section of your presentation to Italian and another to English. PowerPoint will automatically check the text in the correct language.

Accessibility

This tool checks your presentation for accessibility issues, ensuring that your presentation is also usable by people with disabilities. For example, the feature can highlight the lack of alt text for images or issues with colors and contrasts, providing suggestions to make your presentation more inclusive.

- **Suggestions for improvement**: PowerPoint provides tips on how to improve the accessibility of your presentation, such as adding descriptions for images or using more readable fonts.

Paragraphs and text direction

Text direction: This option allows you to change the direction of the text, for example, for languages written from right to left, such as Arabic or Hebrew. It is essential for those who work with multiple languages or international contexts.

Show

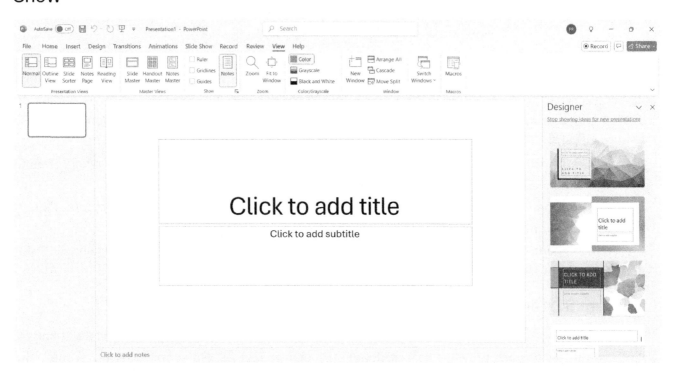

The **View** tab in PowerPoint focuses on the visual and structural aspects of the presentation, offering different display modes to help the user work more effectively. While creating the content and design is essential, how you view it and how elements are arranged on your work screen greatly influences your workflow. From here, you can change the slide view, access specific schemes (such as printouts or notes), activate precision tools such as rulers and grids, and manage Zoom to tailor the view.

How to view the presentation

PowerPoint offers several viewing modes to make it easier to organize, review, and design slides.
- **Standard**: The default view mode shows a slide in the middle of the screen with the slide sequence on the left. In this view, you can work freely on the individual slide and quickly access all the others for quick edits.
- **Structure**: This mode shows the presentation as a structured list of titles and content without images or charts. It is particularly useful for organizing text, quick reviews of the content structure, and editing slide titles and main points in sequence.

- **Slide Sorter**: This tool shows all the thumbnail slides in a grid, allowing you to see the entire flow of the presentation. You can rearrange your slides by dragging and dropping, deleting unnecessary ones, or inserting new slides in the right place. It helps manage your presentation globally and see how the slides are distributed to each other.
- **Notes page**: This page splits the screen, showing the slide at the top and the space for **speaker notes** below. In this mode, you can add comments or landmarks that the audience won't see but will be helpful during the presentation. It's beneficial for presenters who must follow a script or remember specific details for each slide.

Reading mode allows you to view the presentation in full screen but in read-only mode without the toolbar. It's a convenient way to review your presentation, as your audience will see it while quickly returning to editing.

Schematics

Schemas are structural templates that control the appearance of slides, printed sheets, and notes. These templates ensure visual consistency and consistent formatting throughout your presentation.
- **Slide Master**: Changes the **main layout** of the presentation. Each slide is based on a master, so any changes you make to the slide master will automatically be reflected on all linked slides. You can manage global elements such as title placement, fonts, colors, and backgrounds from here.
- **Printed Schema**: This defines how slides will look when printed. You can choose whether to include multiple slides per page, with or without notes, and organize your print to be optimized for your audience's needs or for the presenter.

- **Notes Master**: This option allows you to change the layout of the **speaker notes** pages, which include the slide and space to write notes. It helps organize how this information is presented when printing or in the presenter's view.

Precision Instruments

PowerPoint offers precision tools such as **rulers, grids,** and guides to help you position objects, images, and text accurately within your slides.

- **Ruler**: This section shows a horizontal and vertical ruler that allows you to position objects precisely within the slide. It helps align text, images, and other elements consistently and professionally.
- **Grid**: This button activates an alignment grid on the slide, visible in the background. The grid helps to position objects precisely, especially when you need uniformity in layout. You can also adjust the space between the grid lines to suit your needs.

Guides: Guides are reference lines that you can manually position to help you align and distribute objects on a slide. You can add horizontal and vertical guides, move them, and duplicate them to get precise alignment control.

Zoom

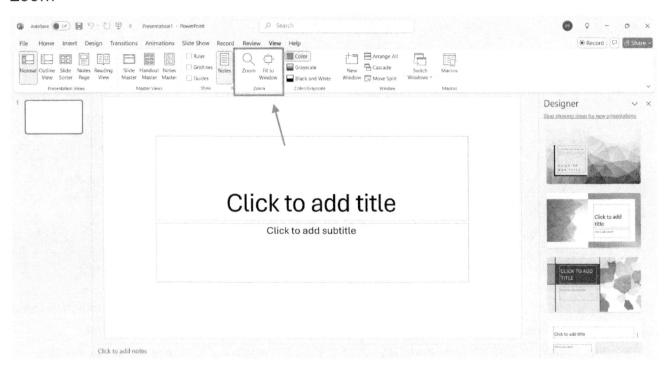

Zoom in or out of the workspace on the slide so you can focus on specific details or see the entire slide in the context of your presentation.

- **Zoom**: Adjusts the magnification level of the current slide. You can choose to zoom in to work on fine details or zoom out to see the entire slide. You can select specific zoom levels (such as 50%, 100%, or 200%) or use manual scrolling for custom zoom.

- **100%**: This function returns the zoom level to the actual size of the slide without zooming in or out.
- **Fit to Window**: This feature automatically fits the slide to the work window, ensuring that the entire slide is visible without the need to scroll.

Macros

This feature allows you **to automate repetitive tasks** by recording and playing back macros. Macros are actions that can be repeated with a single click, making performing complex or repetitive tasks faster. It's an advanced, helpful feature for those who often work with large amounts of data or want to automate formatting or editing tasks.

Other

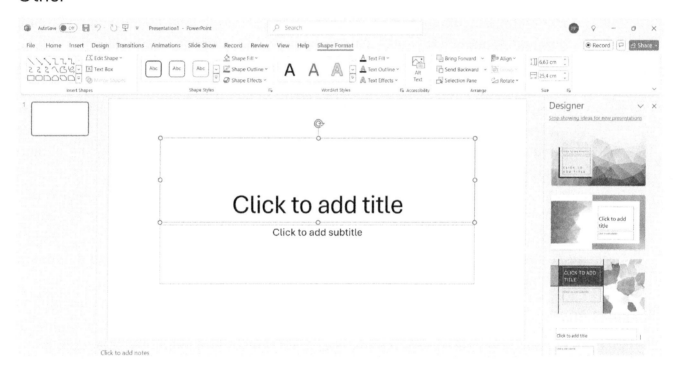

When you select a **specific element in** PowerPoint, such as a picture, shape, chart, or text box, a highlighted **contextual tab** (usually in red) called "More" automatically appears. This tab gives you access to advanced tools to edit the selected element, offering options for customizing various graphic and layout aspects. Depending on the type of object you choose, PowerPoint provides dedicated tools to improve the appearance and arrangement of that element within the slide.
Here's an overview of the key features found in the **More tab**:

Graphic formatting

PowerPoint gives you various formatting options to customize the selected element when you choose an object, such as a **shape**, **picture**, or **text box**.
- **Edges and contours**:

- **Shape Fill**: This option allows you to fill the inside of a shape or text box with a color of your choice. You can choose a solid color, gradient, or image as the fill.
- **Shape Outline**: Change the border's color, thickness, and style around the shape or text box. You can choose from predefined or custom colors, select a different border thickness, and choose solid, dashed, or dotted line styles.
- **Shape Effects**: Add special visual effects such as shadows, reflections, glows, bevels, or 3D rotations to enhance the selected shape or element's depth and visual impact.

Arrangement and layering

PowerPoint provides arrangement tools that let you control the position of an element relative to other objects on the slide.

- **Bring forward/backward**:
  - **Move Forward**: This option moves the selected item higher than the other objects. This is useful when one object is hidden behind another, and you want it to be visible.
  - **Bring Back**: This function moves the selected item behind other objects. It is useful when you want an element in the slide's background.
  - **Bring to Front**: This action moves the selected object to the top layer, making it fully visible above all other objects on the slide.
  - **Send to Background**: Moves the selected object to the lowest layer behind all other objects.
- **Align**: This option allows you to align the selected element with respect to the slide or with respect to other objects. You can align objects to the left, right, center, top, or bottom and distribute them evenly across the slide.
- **Rotate**: This function rotates the selected item clockwise or counterclockwise, applies a 90-degree rotation, or mirrors reflection (horizontal or vertical).

Size and Aspect Ratio

The More tab allows you to change the exact **size** of any selected object to ensure an accurate layout.

- **Width and height**: You can manually set an element's precise width and height by entering specific numeric values. This feature helps ensure consistency across multiple objects or to fit graphics to a predefined space.
- **Lock aspect ratio**: When you change an object's size, you can lock the aspect ratio so that the element retains its original aspect ratio as it is resized. This is especially useful for avoiding warping when resizing images or shapes.

Text Box

When you select a **text box**, you can access advanced options to manage the text and its container.

- **Fit text**: You can choose whether the text inside the box should automatically fit the size of the text box or whether the box should expand to accommodate all the text. This option helps keep your presentation uncluttered and visually consistent.

- **Margins**: Adjust the inner margins of the text box to control the amount of space left between the text and the box's edges. You can customize the margins at the top, bottom, left, and right to get the desired look.
- **Text Orientation**: You can change the orientation of the text within the box, such as from horizontal to vertical, or by rotating it 90 degrees.

Specific formats

Depending on the type of object you select, the **Other** tab may include specialized tools for formatting that item. Some examples include:

- **Image format**: If you select an image, you'll have access to tools to adjust brightness, contrast, and transparency and to add frames, borders, or special effects.
- **Charts**: If you select a chart, PowerPoint offers options to change the chart style, customize the colors of the data series, change the chart layout, and manage data labels.

The **More** tab in PowerPoint gives you fine-grained and precise control over each graphic, allowing you to fully customize your presentation's visual look and feel. You can adjust the borders, fills, size, and arrangement of objects, ensuring that each element is precisely where and how you want it to be. Whether you're working on images, shapes, or text boxes, the **More tab** allows you to easily manage the size, colors, borders, and effects to achieve a professional and visually consistent result.

Animations and transitions

Animations **and transitions** in **Microsoft PowerPoint 2025** are powerful tools that allow you to add dynamism and engagement to your presentations. Applying animations to text, images, and graphic objects can help focus your audience's attention on critical points, while smooth transitions between slides improve the flow of your presentation. In this paragraph, we'll explore how to apply and customize **transitions between slides** and how to create **animation to** make your presentation more interactive and visually appealing.

Applying transitions to slides

Transitions are visual effects as you move from one slide to another. Adding transitions can make switching between different contents in your presentation smoother and less abrupt. PowerPoint 2025 offers a wide range of transitions, from the simplest and most sober to the most elaborate and animated.

Here's how to apply a transition:

- Select the slide to which you want to apply the transition.
- Go to the **Transitions tab** and choose the effect you prefer from the group of options. Some common examples include **Fade**, **Browse**, **Cut,** and **Transform**.
- Once you've chosen a transition, you can customize its duration using the **Duration** options on the same tab. This allows you to control how fast or slow the transition between slides happens.
- You can also add **sounds** or turn on the transition automatically after a certain amount of time, which is useful when the presentation is done without user intervention (such as at kiosks or trade shows).

Transitions can help you keep your audience's attention, but they must be used sparingly. Ideally, you should apply simple, consistent transitions throughout your presentation, using more elaborate effects only in exceptional cases, such as when moving to a new section.

Creating animations for text and objects

In addition to transitions between slides, PowerPoint allows you to animate **individual elements within slides**, such as text, images, charts, shapes, and icons. Animations can be used to gradually introduce a slide's content, keep the audience's attention on one point at a time, or highlight important information. Here are some types of animations available in PowerPoint 2025:

- **Input**: The object appears on the slide dynamically (e.g., **Appearance, Sliding in, Disappearing**).
- **Emphasis**: The object changes shape, color, or size as it is visible on the slide, drawing attention (e.g., **underlining, Magnification**).
- **Exit**: The object disappears from the slide; with effects such as **Fade** or **Fade**.
- **Motion paths**: Move objects along a specific path on the slide.

To apply an animation:

- Select the slide element you want to animate.
- Go to the **Animations tab** and select the desired effect from the group of options.
- You can customize the animation by changing the **direction**, **speed,** and **sequence** (for example, you can make text appear line by line or an image from one side of the slide to the other).

You can also manage the build order through the **Build Pane**, which lets you see all the builds applied to a slide and change their order or timing. You can also use the **Wake After Click** feature to start the animation only when you're ready, giving you more control over the timing of your presentation.

When and how to use animations and transitions

Using animations and transitions should always be considered to keep the presentation professional and effective. Here are some tips for getting the most out of these features:

- **Visual consistency**: Try to maintain consistency in the animations and transitions used. For example, use the same transition effect to move from one section to another and apply similar animations to present related information.
- **Simple animations**: Although PowerPoint offers a wide range of animations, avoiding overdoing them is essential. Animations should be simple and improve understanding of the content, not distract the audience.
- **Pacing Control**: Using animations and transitions allows you to **control the pace** of your presentation. For example, you can introduce critical points from a slide one at a time, keeping your audience's attention high and ensuring that concepts are presented correctly.

Advanced Tips

Once you're familiar with the primary and intermediate features of Microsoft PowerPoint 2025, it's time to explore some **advanced tips** that can elevate the quality of your presentations, making them even more **professional, dynamic,** and **engaging**. These tricks will allow you to optimize your work, improving the effectiveness of communication and the visual impact of the slides.

Techniques to make presentations more effective

An effective presentation is not only aesthetically pleasing, but it can also clearly convey the message to the audience. Here are some advanced techniques for creating presentations that grab attention and make it easier to understand:

- **Minimalism and visual clarity**: Less is more regarding text and images on a slide. Use **a few words** to convey the critical idea and support the text with eye-catching visuals. Pictures and graphics should be supporting tools, not overpower the main message.
- **Smart Highlighting**: PowerPoint allows you **to highlight key points** with animation or formatting effects. You can use **bold, contrasting colors** or **emphasis animations** to highlight important details. However, doing this sparingly is essential so your audience can handle the distractions.
- **Tell a story**: Every presentation should tell a story. Organize your slides logically, as if you were guiding your audience through a journey with a beginning, development, and end. This narrative method helps keep attention high and facilitates understanding concepts.

Using PowerPoint's advanced features

PowerPoint 2025 introduces several advanced features that you can take advantage of to enhance your presentations. Here are some of the most useful:

- **SmartArt**: The **SmartArt** tool automatically transforms simple texts into eye-catching and dynamic charts. You can use it to create **diagrams, workflows, hierarchies**, or **processes**, making complex concepts visually understandable. This feature is accessible from the **Insert** tab > **SmartArt** and offers various customizable templates.
- **Interactive charts**: PowerPoint allows you to create **interactive charts** that change dynamically based on the data you enter. This feature is essential when you need to visualize large amounts of data or present **projections** and **trends**. Charts can be edited in real time and linked directly to Excel spreadsheets, allowing for automatic updates when data changes.
- **Embedded video and audio**: Integrating **multimedia content** such as video or audio into your slides can enrich your presentation, making it more interactive. PowerPoint allows you to insert local video files or directly embed content from platforms like YouTube. You can also record **audio narrations** to guide the audience through the presentation, which is useful for automated or online presentations.

Time and Evidence Management

PowerPoint offers tools to help you rehearse and **control the tempo** of your presentation. These tools are crucial if you need to present within specific time constraints or want your presentation to scroll automatically at a certain speed.

- **Test Timing Tool**: Go to the **Presentation tab** and select **Test Timings** to test the duration of each slide. This allows you to time how much time you spend on each slide and perfectly sync your presentation with your exposure times.
- **Presenter Mode**: PowerPoint offers a **Presenter Mode** that allows you to view notes and preview the next slide without the audience seeing them. This is an excellent tool for keeping your presentation smooth and well-organized, especially during long presentations.

Securing and sharing presentations

Once you're done with your presentation, PowerPoint offers several options to **protect** and **share** your work. You can password-protect your presentation so that only those with the code can edit it or turn it into a PDF file to ensure the layout and content remain the same.

In addition, the **real-time sharing feature** allows you to collaborate with colleagues and workmates on a presentation simultaneously. You can also broadcast your presentation to a remote audience via **Microsoft Teams** or other collaboration platforms.

5. Export and Conversion

PowerPoint 2025 offers a range of options for **exporting** your presentation in various formats. In addition to the classic **PDF** export, you can convert your presentation into an **MP4 video**, which helps you share it online or for automatic presentations. PowerPoint also allows you to export individual **multimedia elements** (images, videos, and audio) directly from the slides, making it easier to reuse content.

6. Microsoft Outlook 2025

Microsoft Outlook 2025 is much more than just an email manager. This updated version of the popular communication tool offers advanced integration with the rest of the **Microsoft Office** suite. It introduces features that make managing emails, calendars, and daily tasks more efficient and productive. Whether managing a full inbox, hosting meetings, or syncing tasks with other Microsoft applications, Outlook 2025 gives you a wide range of tools to streamline your workflow.

Outlook's main strength lies in its ability to centralize everything you need for communication and time management in one place. Not only can you send and receive emails, but you can also organize meetings, create automation rules to optimize your inbox, and seamlessly integrate your work with tools like **Teams, OneNote,** and **Power Automate**. In this chapter, we'll explore Outlook 2025's key features and how they can improve the day-to-day management of your tasks.

Introduction to Outlook 2025

Microsoft Outlook 2025 is much more than just an email client. It is a complete communication platform that integrates email management, appointment scheduling, task management, and collaboration with team members in a single interface. With this release, Microsoft has made significant improvements to Outlook's key features, making it an even more powerful tool for those working in professional or academic environments.

One of Outlook 2025's key features is its ability to centralize all communications and tasks in one place. The ability to manage emails, calendars, and tasks from a single interface not only simplifies daily work but also increases productivity by eliminating the need to constantly switch between different applications. Outlook is designed to be highly customizable, allowing you to tailor it to your specific needs, whether managing a single project or coordinating larger teams.

Critical Features of Outlook 2025

Outlook 2025 stands out for several **advanced features** that make it ideal for individual use and business collaboration environments. Key features include:

- **Smart Inbox**: With features like **Focused Inbox**, Outlook helps you separate essential emails from less relevant ones, ensuring that you focus only on the most meaningful messages. This feature leverages artificial intelligence to automatically analyze your inbox and sort emails by their priority, improving efficiency.
- **Built-in calendars and meetings**: Outlook 2025 calendar is a tool for keeping track of appointments. It is tightly integrated with email and **Microsoft Teams**, making scheduling meetings and video conferences easy with just a few clicks. You can see attendees' availability, send invitations, and attach relevant notes or documents directly from appointments.
- **Full synchronization with Office 365**: One of Outlook 2025's most popular features is its **seamless integration with the rest of the Microsoft Office suite**, such as **Word, Excel, PowerPoint,** and **OneNote**. This means you can easily switch between applications, sync information, and work collaboratively with your team.

A platform for modern work

Outlook 2025 is designed to be at the center of your daily work routine. With tools like **Power Automate**, you can automate repetitive tasks and save valuable time. With its integration capabilities, you can easily connect Outlook with other applications, such as **SharePoint** or third-party software, to handle more complex projects or respond quickly to customer inquiries.

The new Outlook graphical interface is designed to improve **productivity and ease of use**. It features easily accessible commands, greater customization of toolbars, and advanced search capabilities. In addition, **data protection** has been further enhanced with new encryption and authentication features, ensuring that your communications are always secure.

Advanced email management

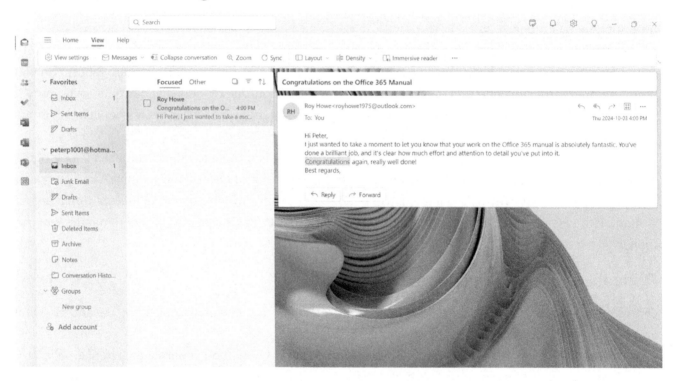

Managing emails is one of the most challenging daily tasks, especially when receiving dozens or hundreds of messages daily. **Microsoft Outlook 2025** is designed to help you manage your inbox more efficiently, allowing you to reduce clutter and focus on the most critical messages. Its advanced features will enable you to organize, automate, and filter emails, making it easy to manage large volumes of messages and keep your inbox tidy.

Focused Inbox

One of Outlook 2025's most valuable features is the **Focused Inbox**, which automatically separates the most critical emails from the less relevant ones. This feature leverages AI to analyze your reading and response patterns, learning which messages are prioritized for you. Emails needing immediate attention are placed in the "Highlighted" tab. In contrast, others remain in the "Other" tab, reducing the risk of missing important messages.

You can turn this feature on or off from the **View** tab and customize the criteria that determine which emails should be considered "Highlighted." This allows you to have complete control over your inbox without having to waste time manually scrolling through hundreds of messages.

Snooze emails

Another feature that improves efficiency is the ability **to sleep emails**. This feature allows you to delay an email from appearing in your inbox until a more convenient time. It's beneficial when you receive messages requiring a response but can't handle them immediately. Snoozing the email will temporarily disappear from your inbox and reappear at the scheduled time, helping you better manage your time and priorities.

To snooze an email, right-click the message and select the **Snooze** option. You can choose a specific time or future date for it to reappear, allowing you to manage emails based on their urgency or importance.

3. Filters and rules for automation

Outlook 2025 allows you to create **custom rules** to automate your inbox management. You can set up rules that automatically move emails to specific folders, mark them as read, or classify them with labels. This lets you keep your inbox organized and minimize your time manually searching and filtering messages.

Here's how to create a rule in Outlook:

- Go to the **Files** tab and select **Manage Rules and Alerts**.
- Create a new rule based on specific criteria, such as the email's sender, subject, or content.
- Define the desired action (e.g., move to a folder, forward, delete) and save the rule.

With this automation, Outlook becomes a virtual assistant that organizes your inbox, allowing you to focus on more urgent and relevant messages.

Labels and categories

Outlook 2025 also allows you **to categorize emails** using custom **labels and categories**. These tools will enable you to flag emails based on the project, priority, or type of action required. You can customize categories with **different colors**, making finding and managing related emails easier.

To apply a category:

- Right-click the desired email and select **Categorize by Categories**.
- You can also create or modify new categories to fit your needs.

This classification system allows you to see your inbox clearly, automatically grouping messages that belong to the same project or require similar actions.

Quick Storage

The **archive** feature in Outlook 2025 allows you to clean your inbox without deleting messages. You can quickly archive emails in a dedicated folder, keeping them accessible in the future but out of your inbox. This tool is useful when you've handled an email but don't want to delete it or need to make room for new messages.

To archive an email, select it and click **Archive** in the toolbar. Archived emails are easily accessible via the search function.

Synchronization with other Office applications

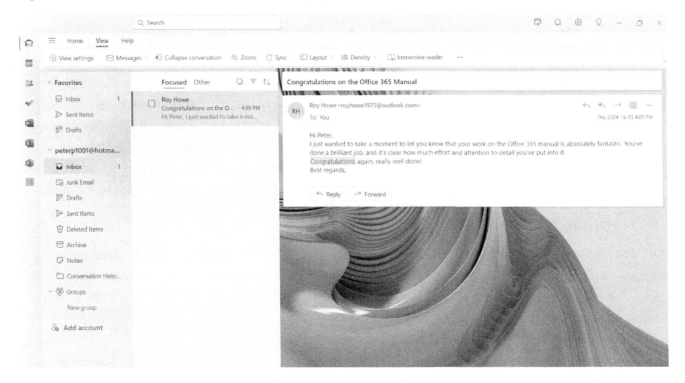

One of **Microsoft Outlook 2025's most powerful features** is its ability to quickly and efficiently manage calendars and **meeting scheduling**. These features allow you to keep track of your commitments and appointments and give you advanced tools for collaborating with your team, syncing events, and hosting virtual meetings. In this paragraph, we'll explore how to use your Outlook calendar to schedule meetings, view colleagues' availability, and manage events professionally.

Built-in calendars

Outlook 2025 gives you a centralized view of all your calendars, whether personal or professional. You can **manage multiple calendars at once**, allowing you to separate work and private commitments but still view them in a single interface to get an overview. This is especially useful for avoiding overlaps between personal and professional commitments.

Each calendar can be customized with **different colors**, helping you quickly differentiate between appointments or events. You can also share your calendars with colleagues to facilitate collaboration and schedule team meetings.

Scheduling meetings

Scheduling **meetings** in Outlook 2025 is simple and intuitive. You can create meeting invitations directly from your calendar, add attendees, and attach meeting documents or notes. One key feature of Outlook is the ability to see the **availability** of participants, so you can schedule the meeting at a time that is convenient for everyone.

Here's how to schedule a meeting in Outlook 2025:

- Go to your **calendar** and click **New Meeting**.
- Add the meeting subject, date, and time.
- Invite attendees by entering their email addresses and selecting the **Scheduling Assistant option** to see when they're available.
- Attach relevant documents or notes and set meeting reminders.

Outlook will send you automatic notifications when attendees accept or decline the invitation, and you can quickly reschedule the meeting if necessary.

Microsoft Teams integration

One of Outlook 2025's most popular features is its **seamless integration with Microsoft Teams**. When scheduling a meeting, you can select the option to turn it into a **video conference using Teams**. This allows participants to join the meeting with the click of a button without having to search for separate links or go through other platforms.

Teams' integration allows you to:

- **Set up video conferencing** directly from Outlook, automatically adding Teams meeting details to the invitation.
- **Synchronize meetings and** chats between the two applications so that information is constantly updated on both platforms.
- **Share files and documents** in real time during the meeting.

This built-in workflow allows you to minimize the steps required to schedule and manage virtual meetings, making the process smoother and more professional.

Automatic scheduling suggestions

Outlook 2025 includes a **Planning Suggestions** tool. This tool uses artificial intelligence to analyze attendee availability and suggest the best times for meetings. It is especially useful when you're having trouble finding a time when everyone is available.

You can access this feature through the Scheduling **Assistant**, which shows you a list of available times for each attendee. Once you select a time, Outlook automatically sends invitations and updates all attendees' calendars.

Sync with other calendars

Outlook 2025 allows you to **synchronize your calendars with other applications** and platforms. You can import and sync events directly into Outlook from external calendars, such as Google Calendar or iCal. This allows you to manage all your appointments on one platform without jumping between different applications.

Synchronization is especially useful for teams working across multiple platforms. It allows **for seamless collaboration** and centralized engagement management.

Tips and shortcuts

Advanced **email management** in **Microsoft Outlook 2025** allows you to optimize and automate many of your daily email-related tasks, saving you valuable time and improving the organization of your inbox. With advanced features like **rules and filters**, **smart folders**, and automation tools, Outlook becomes a potent tool for anyone who works with large volumes of messages or needs fine-grained control over communications.

Automations with rules and filters

One key feature of advanced email management in Outlook 2025 is the ability to create **custom rules** that automate the processing of incoming messages. Rules allow you to set specific criteria to automatically sort emails, such as moving them to dedicated folders, applying labels, or marking them as read based on the message's sender, subject, or content.

For example, receive regular reports or newsletters. You can create a rule that automatically moves these messages to a separate folder, thus keeping your inbox clean and tidy. You can also set up rules to prioritize certain emails, such as messages from important customers or colleagues so that they stand out from others.

To create a rule in Outlook 2025:

- Go to the **Files** tab and select **Manage Rules and Alerts**.
- Create a new rule based on criteria of your choice, such as sender, keyword, or message size.
- Define Outlook's action (for example, move to a specific folder, forward, or delete).

With this automation, you can minimize the time spent manually managing your inbox and focus on more relevant emails.

Using Smart Folders

Intelligent **folders** in Outlook 2025 are another powerful tool for keeping your inbox organized. These folders work as "dynamic filters" that automatically group emails based on specific criteria without physically moving the messages. For example, you can create a smart folder that shows only unread emails or includes all emails from a particular project or client, regardless of the folder in which they were stored. Smart folders allow you to quickly access the necessary messages without manually searching dozens of folders. You can also set up multiple intelligent folders to manage various workflows simultaneously.

Automation with Power Automate

Outlook 2025 seamlessly integrates **Power Automate**, a tool that allows you to create automated workflows between different Microsoft and third-party applications. With Power Automate, you can automate a wide range of tasks, such as automatically replying to certain emails, storing attachments in **OneDrive,** or sending notifications when you receive emails from specific senders.

For example, suppose you regularly receive emails with necessary attachments. In that case, you can set up a workflow that automatically stores them in a OneDrive folder, eliminating the need to manually download files. You can also create a workflow that sends you a notification on **Microsoft Teams** whenever you receive an urgent email, allowing you to stay updated in real-time, even when you don't have direct access to Outlook.

Power Automate is particularly useful for those who manage **repetitive tasks** and want to reduce the time spent on mechanical operations. It allows even more efficient email management when integrated with the rest of the Microsoft suite.

Custom folders and categories

In addition to rules and automation, Outlook 2025 allows you to manage emails in an advanced way through **custom folders** and **categories**. You can create dedicated folders for each project, client, or topic and move emails manually or automatically using the rules you've configured. Folders can be structured hierarchically, allowing you to better organize the content of your mail.

Categories, on the other hand, are useful for **labeling** emails with colors and keywords, making it easier to locate relevant messages quickly. For example, you can assign a red category to urgent emails, a blue category to messages related to ongoing projects, and so on. This visual classification system makes it easier to identify messages, especially when working with large volumes of emails.

Quick Responses and Actions

For those looking to save time, Outlook 2025 also introduces **quick actions**, which allow you to reply to an email or perform other everyday actions (such as archiving or deleting) with a single click directly from your inbox. These quick actions can be customized to suit your needs, simplifying routine tasks and making the email management process much more efficient.

You can configure these actions from the **Outlook Settings** tab, choosing from the default actions or creating your own to fit your workflow.

Adding Multiple Accounts

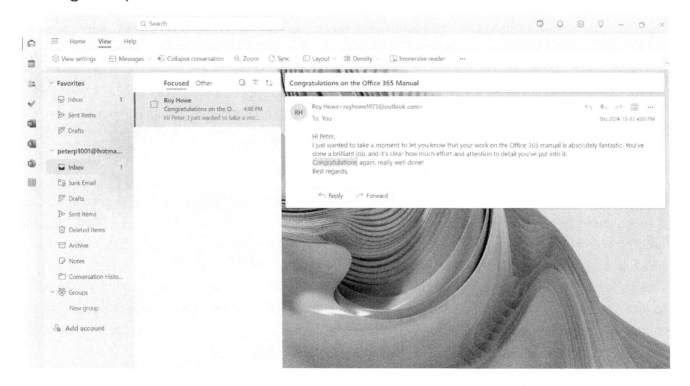

One of the most valuable aspects of **Microsoft Outlook** is the ability to **manage multiple email accounts** from one place. This is especially beneficial if you use several email addresses, whether for personal or professional purposes. Whether you have a business and a personal email address or multiple accounts for various projects, Outlook integrates them into a single interface, allowing you to monitor and manage all your mail without logging in to each provider individually.

How to add a new email account on Outlook

1. **Open Outlook** and click File in the top left.
2. Select **Add account**.
3. A window will appear where you need to enter your **email address**. Enter the address of the new account you want to add and click **Connect**.
4. Depending on the provider of your new email account (for example, Gmail, Yahoo, or a business account), you'll be asked to enter your **password** or authenticate via a **confirmation link**.
5. After authentication, Outlook will automatically set up your new account. You can choose to set it as the default or keep it separate from your other addresses.

Once you've completed this process, you'll see the newly added account in the Outlook sidebar and all your other mailboxes. From here, you can manage all your emails from a single interface without logging in to each account individually on different websites.

Benefits of having multiple accounts integrated into Outlook

Integrating multiple email addresses into **Outlook allows** you to always keep track of your email without the hassle of **logging in** to each provider. This feature makes your workflow much more efficient, especially if you need to quickly switch between inboxes.

In addition, thanks to Outlook's intuitive interface and integration with the entire **Microsoft Office** ecosystem, you have advanced email management tools. For example, you can take advantage of features like custom rule creation, quick archive, and calendar management, all within a single environment, improving your productivity and keeping all your correspondence organized.

In this way, Outlook not only allows you to simplify the management of your emails but also offers you the opportunity to do so with the **graphic and functional power** of the Microsoft Office package, making the experience much smoother and more professional.

7. Microsoft Teams 2025

Microsoft Teams 2025 is the heart of modern collaboration, especially for remote or distributed teams. Teams are not just a tool for virtual meetings but a real **work hub** where team members can communicate, collaborate on documents, plan events, and manage projects in real time. This release of Teams introduces new tools and enhancements that make teamwork easier, communication smoother, and project management more efficient.

This chapter explores setting up and organizing a team, scheduling virtual meetings, managing files and conversations, and making the most of integrations with **OneDrive**, **SharePoint,** and other Microsoft apps. In addition, we will focus on **tips for remote work**, an increasingly relevant aspect for modern organizations, providing techniques to optimize remote collaboration and maintain high productivity.

Get started with Microsoft Teams.

Microsoft Teams 2025 is confirmed as one of the leading tools for business collaboration and teamwork management, especially useful in an era where remote and hybrid work is increasingly becoming the norm. Initially born as a messaging and video conferencing platform, Teams has become a true **collaborative work hub** over time, thanks to its integration with the entire **Microsoft 365**suite and its ability to support a wide range of third-party applications.

Teams' core strength lies in their ability **to centralize** their communications and activities in a single digital environment, eliminating the need to jump between different applications. Whether it's conversations, **video conferencing, file sharing**, or **project management**, Teams enables real-time collaboration and a faster and more seamless workflow.

Why use Microsoft Teams 2025?

This release of Microsoft Teams introduces several enhancements that make it even more flexible and powerful for teams of all sizes, from small businesses to large organizations. Teams 2025 was designed to simplify teamwork, allowing team members to collaborate **from anywhere** and **in real-time**. Its advanced features not only make communication easier but also improve productivity with task management tools and automation.

Here are some of the key reasons why Teams 2025 is a critical resource for organizations:

- **All-in-one platform**: Teams is not only a tool for virtual meetings but also offers the ability to manage **documents**, **projects**, and **communications** from a single interface.
- **Seamless integration with Microsoft 365**: Teams can work in close synergy with other applications such as **Word, Excel, PowerPoint, OneNote**, and **OneDrive**. This allows you to work on documents simultaneously without leaving the platform.
- **Centralized file management**: Teams make organizing, sharing, and collaborating on files easy and secure. Every document uploaded to Teams channels is accessible to all authorized members, and changes happen in real-time.
- **Video conferencing and virtual meetings**: Teams support meetings with up to hundreds of participants, with screen sharing, chat, and automatic session recording options.

Microsoft Teams for modern work

In today's world, where remote and hybrid work is becoming integral to company culture, Microsoft Teams is a valuable ally. It is a tool designed to address the growing need **for remote collaboration** by providing a centralized platform that allows team members to stay connected and in sync at all times.

With the increasing integration of tools such as **Microsoft Teams Rooms** and **Surface Hub**, Teams also supports hybridization between physical and virtual environments, making meetings more accessible and inclusive, no matter where participants are located. Using Teams helps not only improve internal communication but also facilitates external collaborations with **secure sharing features** with customers or partners.

Additionally, Teams supports many **apps and integrations** that allow teams to customize the platform to their specific needs. From project management to data analysis, you can create a digital workplace tailored to your team's needs, improving productivity and collaboration.

How to set up and organize a team

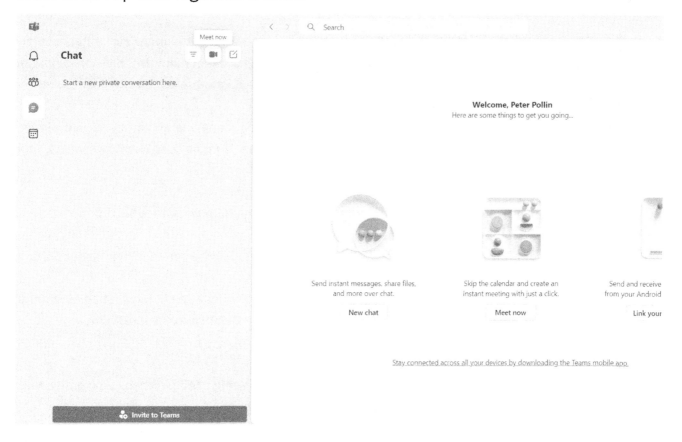

Setting up and organizing a team in **Microsoft Teams 2025** is simple yet essential to ensuring everyone on your team can collaborate efficiently. Organizing a team is the first step in creating a collaborative work environment where communication and task management can run smoothly. Microsoft Teams allows you to create structured teams with dedicated channels and configure permissions and access according to the needs of the project or organization.

Create a new team

Organizing collaborative work starts with creating a team in Microsoft Teams 2025. You can choose to create a team from scratch or rely on **pre-built templates** offered by the platform, such as teams for projects, departments, classes (for academic use), or corporate workgroups. Each team is designed to be a collection of people working together on a common goal, such as a specific project or business division. Here's how to create a team in a few steps:

- Open Microsoft Teams and select **Create Team**.
- You can create a team **from scratch** or **based on an existing Office 365 group** (for example, an email group already set up).
- Enter the team's name and a short description, then decide whether the team will be **public** (accessible to everyone in the organization) or **private** (only invited members can join).
- Invite team members by entering their email addresses or selecting them from your business address book.

Organize channels

Each team created in Microsoft Teams 2025 can be further divided into **channels**. Channels are workspaces dedicated to specific topics, projects, or tasks within the broader team. This division facilitates targeted communication, allowing team members to discuss and collaborate on relevant issues without interfering with unrelated discussions.

For example, a marketing team might have separate channels for managing social media, developing advertising campaigns, and analyzing data. Each channel can contain conversations, files, and applications relevant only to that project or topic.

When organizing channels, it's essential to:

- Create **clear and relevant** channels, so members know immediately where to find information and participate in appropriate discussions.
- **Customize channel permissions**, making some channels **private** for sensitive discussions or small subgroups of team members.
- **Add specific applications** within channels, such as project management tools (such as **Planner** or **Trello**) or shared documents that can be edited directly in **OneDrive** or **SharePoint**.

Configure access and security settings

Configuring access settings and security is a crucial aspect of organizing a team. When you create a team in Microsoft Teams 2025, you have control over who can access channels, edit content, and view files. Access settings can be configured at the team and individual channel levels, ensuring only authorized individuals can view and participate in sensitive discussions.

Here are some tips for setting up team security correctly:

- **Set custom access levels** for team members. You can appoint members with owner (with complete control) or **participant** (limited access) roles.
- Use channel-level **permission management** to ensure that certain members can only access specific information.

- Enable two-factor authentication (2FA) to secure team access and prevent unauthorized access.

Invite external guests

Another powerful feature of Microsoft Teams 2025 is the ability to invite **guests from outside** the team. These can be customers, vendors, or temporary collaborators who need to participate in certain discussions or access specific files. Guest access is restricted and controlled; you can decide which files or conversations you want to make accessible.

To invite a guest:
- Go to **the team settings** and select **Manage Team**.
- Please enter the email address of the external collaborator and submit it.
- Configure permissions for the guest, deciding which channels and files can be viewed.

Task Management and Tracking

Once your team is set up, Microsoft Teams 2025 allows you **to monitor activities and** track all interactions, from conversations to shared documents. Built-in analytics tools give you detailed reports on team usage, member participation, and file interaction, so you always have control over how work is done and managed.

Scheduling and managing virtual meetings

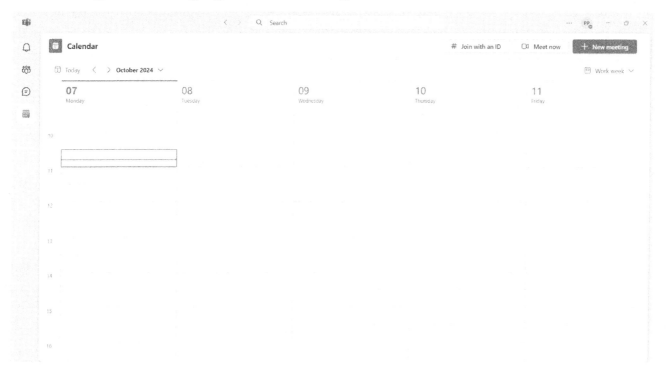

Virtual meetings are vital to **Microsoft Teams 2025**, which offers advanced tools for scheduling, managing, and conducting remote meetings efficiently. Teams' ability to organize online meetings quickly and easily makes It the ideal tool for geographically distributed teams or those working remotely. It allows real-time communication without the need to meet physically. Teams 2025 offers a range of features to manage **video conferencing, real-time chat, screen sharing,** and much more.

115

Scheduling a virtual meeting

Organizing a meeting in **Microsoft Teams is** very simple. You can do it directly from the Teams interface or through the integration with **Outlook**. Teams allow you to schedule recurring or one-time meetings and invite participants both inside and outside your organization. In addition, thanks to the integration with the calendar, you can have an overview of the participants' availability and select a time that is convenient for everyone.

Here's how to schedule a meeting in Microsoft Teams:

- Go to the **Calendar tab** and select **New Meeting**.
- Enter the meeting title, date, and time.
- Add attendees by entering their email addresses and choosing to include external members.
- You can also attach important documents or notes to the meeting invitation so attendees can prepare in advance.

Once scheduled, the meeting will automatically sync to your Outlook and Teams calendar, allowing attendees to receive reminders and join the meeting with a single click.

Conducting a virtual meeting

Microsoft Teams 2025 offers several tools to facilitate collaboration and communication during the virtual meeting. Video **conferences** can be conducted with up to hundreds of participants, and Teams offers **high-definition video quality** with adjustment options to ensure that the connection is stable even in environments with limited bandwidth.

During the meeting, you can:

- **Share your screen** to show presentations, documents, or applications to participants.
- **Record the meeting** to archive it and allow those who couldn't attend to review it later.
- Use **real-time chat** to send messages and share links or files without interrupting your voice conversation.
- **Create** breakout rooms for participants to discuss in small groups before rejoining the central meeting.

Teams also includes **annotation tools** and **digital whiteboards**, allowing you to collaborate on documents or take notes during meetings in real-time.

Meeting Recording and Reporting

A handy feature of Microsoft Teams is the ability to **record meetings**. This feature allows you to create a complete copy of the meeting, including the videos, audio, chat, and shared presentations. Recordings are automatically stored in **OneDrive** or SharePoint, depending on your organization's settings. They can be shared with team members or saved for future reference.

After the meeting ends, Teams also generates an **attendance report**, which allows you to see who attended, how long they stayed, and what time they left the meeting. This report can be useful for tracking attendance at team meetings.

Outlook Integration for Scheduling

The tight integration between Microsoft Teams and **Outlook** allows you to schedule meetings directly from your Outlook calendar. You can also add meeting details and attendees and attach relevant files. This feature makes it easy for team members to see the meeting in their calendars, receive notifications, and join it without searching for separate links or invitations.

When you create a meeting in Outlook, you can select the **Add Teams Meeting** option, and all the connection information will be automatically filled into the invitation. This eliminates the need to manually copy meeting links or create separate invitations in Teams.

Hybrid Meetings and Teams Rooms

With hybrid work becoming more common, Microsoft Teams supports hosting **hybrid meetings**, where some participants are in the office while others participate remotely. **Teams Rooms** is a solution that integrates physical conference rooms with Teams technology, seamlessly connecting in-person and remote participants.

Teams Rooms are equipped with advanced cameras and microphones that allow all participants to clearly see and hear who is speaking, regardless of location. This technology helps to reduce the distance between remote and in-office teams, improving collaboration and participation.

Managing conversations and files

Effective **conversation** and **file management are** one of the pillars on which **Microsoft Teams 2025** is built, making it a central tool for day-to-day collaboration within teams. Teams are not limited to being a video conferencing platform; they also serve as a hub for all text communication and file sharing between team members. The platform seamlessly integrates chat, group discussions, and file-sharing tools, allowing everyone to stay up-to-date and collaborate without external applications.

Real-time conversations

Conversations in Microsoft Teams can occur either at the **private chat** level between two people or within **team channels**, where all project members can participate. This flexibility allows you to keep communications separate based on context, reducing noise and ensuring that every conversation remains relevant to the participants.

- **Private** chats: Private chats are useful for direct communication between two or more team members. You can start a conversation with the click of a button, exchange messages in real time, send files, or even start a video call directly from the chat.
- **Team channels**: You can set up different **channels** for thematic or project-specific discussions within each team you create in Teams. Conversations in channels are visible to all channel members, which makes it easier to collaborate on relevant topics and access previous information.

Teams allows you to follow conversations effectively by using **mentions (@)** that directly notify a specific team member or the entire group. This way, you can be sure that your messages reach the right people quickly without the risk of them being overlooked.

File sharing and management

One of Microsoft Teams' key features is its ability to **share and manage files** within chats and channels. Each team and channel has a dedicated file area where members can upload, edit, and collaborate on documents in real-time. This eliminates the need to email files or worry about keeping track of the most up-to-date versions.

Key file-sharing features in Teams include:

- **Document uploads**: You can upload files directly to a channel or private chat, making them instantly available to all participants. Teams support many file formats, including **Word documents**, **Excel**, **PowerPoint**, PDF, and others.
- **Real-time editing**: Thanks to the integration with **OneDrive** and **SharePoint**, files shared in Teams can be edited by multiple people at the same time. Each team member can open the document directly from Teams and make changes that will be instantly synced for everyone.
- **Automatic versioning**: Teams automatically track previous versions of files, allowing you to quickly retrieve older versions if needed. This feature is handy when multiple people collaborate on a document and a change must be reverted.

Research and organize conversations

With the increasing volume of messages and files within teams, Teams 2025 has boosted its **search and organization capabilities** to help you quickly find relevant information. The Teams search engine allows you to search within chats, **channels, and files**, quickly retrieving essential messages or documents rapidly, even in large teams.

You can search using **keywords**, team member names, or advanced filters to narrow your search to specific conversations, files, or dates. Additionally, you can **pin** essential conversations or files to the top of channels, ensuring critical information is always easily accessible.

4. OneDrive and SharePoint integration

Another crucial aspect of file management in Teams is its tight integration with **OneDrive** and **SharePoint**. These two cloud storage tools ensure your files are always accessible, secure, and well-organized. When you upload a file to a Teams channel, it's automatically stored in **SharePoint** for that team, making it easy to access documents at any time and from any device.

For private conversations or personal files, Teams uses **OneDrive**, where you can securely organize, share, and edit files. This automatic synchronization between Teams, OneDrive, and SharePoint ensures that your files are always up-to-date and you can collaborate in real-time without worrying about sending multiple copies.

Security settings and permissions on files

Microsoft Teams allows you to control **file permissions** to ensure that only the appropriate people can access and edit shared documents. When you upload a file, you can decide who has permission to edit it, who can only view it, and whether it should be protected by additional layers of security. This is especially useful for projects that involve **external collaborators** or when dealing with sensitive files.

You can easily manage permissions directly in Teams or through OneDrive and SharePoint, where you can set specific access levels for files or folders, add passwords, or enable two-factor authentication for added security.

Remote Work Tips

 Remote work has become an established reality in many organizations, and **Microsoft Teams 2025** is one of the most effective tools for facilitating remote collaboration. Working remotely presents specific challenges, such as maintaining a high level of communication and coordination between team members who do not share a physical space. Teams offer a range of tools and features that help remote workers stay connected, productive, and in sync with the rest of the team.

This section will provide some **practical tips** on using Microsoft Teams to improve your remote workflow, optimize communication, and manage time effectively.

Establish clear communication channels

When working remotely, it's essential to establish clear and well-organized communication channels. Teams allow you to create **topic channels** within a team to ensure that discussions are broken down into specific topics and that communications stay visible.

Here are some strategies for making the most of channels:

- **Dedicate a channel to each major project or task**: By separating discussions, team members can focus on topics relevant to their work without being overwhelmed by irrelevant conversations.
- **Create a "social" or "non-formal" channel**: This can improve personal interaction between team members, even if they are working remotely. Teams can use this space for lighter conversations, share informal updates, and strengthen group cohesion.
- **Use mentions (@):** When you need to grab the attention of a team member or the entire group, use mentions to notify specific individuals or the whole team, preventing critical information from being overlooked.

Schedule regular meetings

Scheduling **regular meetings** is crucial for keeping everyone on the same page, especially in a remote work setting. Microsoft Teams 2025 makes it easy to schedule virtual meetings through its built-in calendar and sync them with **Outlook**.

Some tips for managing virtual meetings in the best possible way:

- **Short but frequent meetings**: It's helpful to schedule short, regular meetings, such as daily stand-up meetings or weekly updates, to keep everyone informed of progress and ongoing activities.

- **Clear agenda**: Set a clear agenda for each meeting and share documents or talking points with attendees ahead of time to make the meeting more effective.
- **Use the recording feature**: Meeting recordings can be especially useful for members who can't attend in real-time. They are automatically stored in OneDrive or SharePoint and can be reviewed at any time.

Collaborate on documents in real-time

A key aspect of remote work is **real-time collaboration** on documents and files. Teams are tightly integrated with **OneDrive, SharePoint, Word, Excel,** and **PowerPoint**, allowing teams to work on the same documents simultaneously without version issues.

Here's how to optimize document collaboration:
- **Real-time sharing and editing**: Team members can access files shared in channels or chats, edit them simultaneously, and instantly see changes made by others.
- **Comments and tracked changes**: Use commenting tools within Word, Excel, or PowerPoint to leave feedback or suggestions directly in documents, improving your collaborative workflow.
- **Automatic versioning**: Teams automatically maintains file version history, making it easy to retrieve previous versions if needed.

Time and task management

Working remotely requires careful time management and effective task organization. Teams offer a range of **task management** tools, which can be used to coordinate work among team members and track progress.

Some helpful tools include:
- **Planner**: This Microsoft Teams tool allows you to create **task lists**, assign tasks to team members, and track the progress of each task.
- **To-Do**: Microsoft To-Do is perfect for managing **personal tasks** within Teams. It allows you to create reminders and organize your daily priorities.
- **Timelines and deadlines**: Set deadlines for tasks and use the Teams calendar to keep track of scheduled tasks and meetings, ensuring that work is progressing on schedule.

A synchronization of communications

Remote work often involves collaboration between team members in **different time zones**, so asynchronous communication becomes crucial. Teams allow you to keep team members updated even when they're not online simultaneously.

Asynchronous chat: Conversations can continue even when participants are not online simultaneously, as messages and files remain available to view and respond to at any time.

Video messages and updates: In addition to text conversations, Teams allows you to send **video messages** or record short updates, which can be useful for explaining complex concepts or providing more detailed feedback.

8. Microsoft OneNote 2025

Microsoft OneNote 2025 is an essential tool for **managing digital notes** for personal or professional use. OneNote helps you organize, structure, and share information clearly and efficiently, making it easy to collaborate on projects, manage information, and synchronize across devices. With the growing need for digital tools that integrate notes, projects, and tasks into a single platform, OneNote stands out for its flexibility and versatility.

OneNote 2025 offers advanced tools that allow you **to structure your notebooks**, create custom sections, **sync information across** different devices, and **collaborate in real time** with colleagues. This chapter will explore the main features of OneNote in detail, focusing on how to optimize note management, integrate them with other applications, and improve work organization.

Get started with OneNote

Microsoft OneNote 2025 is one of the most versatile and powerful applications for **managing digital notes**. It is designed to simplify the process of collecting, organizing, and sharing information. OneNote is ideal for both personal and professional use, thanks to its ability to adapt to different needs:

- Taking notes during a meeting
- Gathering ideas for a project
- Organizing study resources
- Even planning an event

The basic structure of OneNote is like that of a traditional notebook but with the added power of digital, allowing **unlimited flexibility** in managing notes. The 2025 version introduces significant improvements in terms of synchronization, integration, and collaboration tools, making the app even more useful for work teams and professionals who need a virtual space to efficiently collect and organize ideas.

What makes OneNote unique?

One of the things that makes OneNote particularly interesting is its ability to **support multiple data formats**. It's not limited to simple blocks of text: you can insert images, tables, freehand drawings, links, audio, and video files, making it an actual **digital container** of all your information. This allows you to collect data from different sources and organize it logically and personally in your notebooks.

Here are some of the key benefits of using OneNote:

- **Organizational flexibility**: You can create **notebooks**, **sections,** and **pages**, allowing you to break down and organize information based on the projects, themes, or categories you want.
- **Accessibility anywhere**: OneNote 2025 automatically syncs your notes across all your devices. Whether working from your computer, smartphone, or tablet, you'll always have access to your information.
- **Real-time collaboration**: OneNote allows you to work closely with your colleagues or collaborators, **edit the** same notes simultaneously, and share information in real-time.
- **Advanced search**: OneNote's search feature is compelling. It allows you to quickly find information within your notes, searching written notes, images, PDF files, and even audio recordings.

An intuitive and integrated work environment

OneNote is not only an information-gathering tool but also designed to improve **personal and team productivity**. Its integration with the entire **Microsoft 365 suite** perfectly complements tools such as **Outlook**, **Teams**, and **OneDrive**. For example, you can easily link your notes to calendar events, create meeting notes directly from Outlook emails, or share your notebooks on Teams to enable seamless collaboration between team members.

Thanks to this integration, OneNote stands out as a true **information control center**. It allows you to centralize all the resources and communications related to your projects without constantly switching between applications.

An application for every context

OneNote 2025 is designed for use in a wide range of contexts. Whether you're a **student**, a **professional,** or a **team leader**, you'll find its features useful for managing information efficiently. You can create **to-do lists**, plan projects, organize brainstorming sessions, or even collect research and articles that you find online.

For students, OneNote offers the ability **to organize lecture notes**, insert freehand images or annotations, and create links between different sections to improve the flow of information. Professionals use OneNote to **manage meetings**, create reports and project notes, or collaborate in real time with colleagues. OneNote is an excellent planning tool for team leaders, as it allows you to track your team's progress and centralize resources.

Advanced clipboard management

One of the standout features of **Microsoft OneNote 2025** is its ability to help you **structure and organize your notes** logically and efficiently, making it easier to collect, categorize, and retrieve information. The **notebooks**, **sections,** and **pages** system allows you to organize your notes by projects, topics, or priorities, providing an extremely versatile information management experience.

1. Notebooks: The Basic Structure

The concept of a **notebook** in OneNote reflects a traditional notebook with much more powerful organizational potential. A notebook is a collection of related information. It can manage notes from meetings, work projects, school lessons, or personal notes.

When you create a new notebook, you can give it a name that reflects its content (for example, "Work Projects," "Marketing Lessons," "Personal Plan"). Each notebook can contain **sections** and **pages** that allow you to further break down the information.

- **Notebooks per project**: You can create a notebook for each project you're working on. For example, a marketing team might have a notebook dedicated to a specific campaign, with sections for every aspect of the strategy (social media, advertising, market research, etc.).
- **Topic Blocks**: Students can create notebooks for each subject of study, with sections dedicated to lectures, projects, exams, or personal notes.

Sections: Organizing Information into Chapters

OneNote **sections** work like the dividers in a traditional notebook, breaking the notebook into specific topics. Each section can contain several **pages** on which you can jot down your ideas and information. Sections can be used to keep your notes well-organized and easily accessible.

Some ways to organize sections include:

- **Themes or topics**: If you're working on a complex project, you can create sections for each key aspect. For example, a project management notebook might have sections such as "Schedule," "Goals," "Timelines," "Budget," and "Deliverable Reports."
- **Time organization**: If you use OneNote to take notes in meetings or classes, you should create sections based on dates or weeks to keep your information in an orderly timeline.
- **Custom categories**: OneNote allows you to create sections to organize your work according to your needs. For example, you can have a section for "Personal Notes," one for "Ongoing Projects," one for "Long-Term Goals," and so on.

Pages and subpages: Detailing information

OneNote **pages** are where you take your notes. Each page can be used for a specific topic within a section. You can add text, images, tables, links, and much more, allowing you to collect all kinds of relevant information.

A helpful feature is creating **subpages to organize** the information further. For example, suppose you're working on a large project. In that case, you can create a page for each phase and subpages for more specific details, such as individual assignments or meeting notes.

- **Meeting pages**: A team that uses OneNote for weekly meetings might have a page for each meeting, with subpages for specific topics discussed or actions to take.
- **Project pages**: If you're working on a multi-phase project, you can create a page for each phase and use subpages for operational details, progress notes, or analytical data.

Labels and categories: Organize and retrieve information quickly

Labels in OneNote 2025 allow you to further organize your notes by applying tags that can be used to **categorize information** and find it quickly. You can add labels to specific notes to categorize ideas, to-dos, questions to review, or important reminders.

Some of the most common labels include:
- **To-Do**: An excellent label for creating to-do lists right on your pages.
- **Necessary**: Use this label to highlight critical information that needs to be reviewed or requires immediate action.
- **Questions**: This label helps mark parts of your notes containing questions or points that need clarification.

Using labels allows you to quickly search and retrieve information within the notebook. You can perform label-specific searches or view all notes labeled with a specific category.

Using Templates for a Consistent Structure

OneNote 2025 offers several **page templates** that allow you to maintain a **consistent structure** in your notes. You can use pre-made templates for meetings, projects, or lesson plans or create and save your own custom templates based on your specific needs.

This is especially useful when repeating the same format for every meeting or project. For example, you can create a template for a meeting that includes sections for goals, attendees, notes, and actions to take so that each new meeting will have the same organizational structure.

How to share and collaborate on notes and projects

One of **Microsoft OneNote 2025's most powerful features** is its ability to make it easy to **share and collaborate on** notes and projects. OneNote lets you work on shared notebooks in real time, making it easy

124

to collaborate with colleagues, classmates, or external partners without having to send constant email updates or manage multiple versions of documents. In this paragraph, we'll explore sharing notebooks, collaborating with others, and managing permissions to ensure secure and efficient collaboration.

Sharing notebooks

With **OneNote 2025**, you can easily share an entire notebook or individual sections with other people. This is especially useful for group projects, where everyone on the team needs access to the same documents or information. Sharing in OneNote is done through **OneDrive** or **SharePoint**, ensuring that notebooks are accessible online and synced automatically.

To share a notebook, follow these steps:

- Go to **File > Share** and select whether you want to share the notebook or a specific section.
- Enter the email addresses of the people you want to share the notebook with.
- Choose whether to grant **edit** or **view-only permissions** to each participant.
- Send the invitation. Recipients will be notified and can access the notebook through their Microsoft account.

Sharing happens in real-time: every change made by one of the participants is immediately updated in the notebook, eliminating the risk of creating duplicate versions or losing information.

Real-time collaboration

Once a notebook is shared, **OneNote 2025 allows** multiple people to work on the same document simultaneously. This is especially useful for collaborative projects, brainstorming, meetings, or lesson plans, where several people can add notes, comments, or reviews in real-time.

Key collaboration features include:

- **Concurrent changes**: All participants can see the changes made by other members in real time. For example, in a meeting, several members can add notes simultaneously, and each will see the others' additions without having to refresh the page.
- **Teams and Outlook integration**: You can integrate your notebooks with **Microsoft Teams**, making it easy to collaborate on projects directly within a channel. Similarly, you can take meeting notes directly from **Outlook**, linking them to specific calendar events.
- **Comments and feedback**: Participants can add comments or suggestions directly to the pages, making it easier to communicate about specific topics or sections of notes.

Permit and security management

When you share a notebook, it's important to **control who can view or edit** the content. **OneNote 2025 lets** you manage the **permissions** of each person you share the notebook with. You can decide whether to give read-only access to prevent accidental edits or allow all participants to add and edit notes.

Here are some of the permission management options:

- **View vs. edit**: You can grant view-only access if you want your colleagues or collaborators to only be able to read the information and not edit it. This is useful for important documents or reference notes.
- **Advanced permission management**: Using **SharePoint** or **OneDrive for Business**, you can have more granular control over permissions by setting specific permissions for individual sections or pages.
- **Password protection of sections**: To protect sensitive information, you can add a **password** to specific sections of your notebooks, preventing unauthorized access.

Version History

A valuable feature of OneNote for collaboration is version **history**. Whenever a team member edits a page or section, OneNote maintains a history of the changes, allowing you to revert to previous versions if necessary. This gives you peace of mind, knowing you will always retain important information due to mistakes or accidental changes.

To access version history:

- Right-click the page you want and select **Version History**.
- You can view the changes you've made and, if necessary, revert to a previous page version.

Integration with other applications for smoother collaboration

OneNote integrates seamlessly with other applications in the Microsoft suite, such as **Teams, Outlook,** and **SharePoint**, making collaboration even more effortless. For example, you can:

- **Link meeting notes to Outlook events**: When you join a meeting, you can create a notebook linked to the Outlook calendar event directly in OneNote, ensuring that all your notes are centralized and easily accessible.
- **Embed notebooks in Teams**: OneNote can be pinned as a tab in a Teams channel, allowing team members to quickly access notes and collaborate in real-time without leaving the Teams environment.
- **SharePoint integration**: If you work with **SharePoint**, OneNote allows you to save and share your notebooks within a SharePoint document library, making it easy to centrally store and manage your company files.

Advanced clipboard management

Microsoft OneNote 2025 offers advanced tools for efficiently managing and organizing notes, making it critical for professionals and students who want to keep track of complex projects, meetings, or personal information. In this section, we'll explore how to use OneNote's advanced features to sync notes across devices, manage sections and pages efficiently, and integrate OneNote with other applications in the Microsoft suite for an optimized work experience.

1. Sync between devices

One of the most valuable features of OneNote is the ability to **automatically sync** your notebooks across all your devices, ensuring that your information is always up-to-date and accessible wherever you are. Whether you're working from your office computer, a tablet on the go, or your smartphone, you can continue to take notes and edit your notes without having to manually transfer files or documents.

- **Real-time access**: Changes made on one device are immediately visible on all other devices linked to your Microsoft account. This ensures you can seamlessly switch between working on your PC, tablet, or smartphone.
- **Offline mode**: OneNote also allows you to work offline. If you don't have an internet connection, you can still edit your notes and sync them automatically when you're back online.
- **OneDrive and SharePoint**: Notebooks are stored in **OneDrive** or **SharePoint**. You can access them from anywhere and on any device connected to your Microsoft account. This system ensures the security of your notes, which are always saved in the cloud.

Efficient use of sections

As mentioned in the previous paragraph, OneNote sections allow you to divide your notebooks into logical categories, making it easier to organize your information. In addition to simply creating sections, some advanced techniques can improve your note management.

- **Colored sections**: You can assign **different colors** to sections to help you quickly identify the categories or projects they belong to. This visual technique is helpful for complex projects or managing multiple topics in a single notebook.
- **Sections and subsections**: If you're working on a project that requires a more detailed breakdown, you can create **subsections** to keep the information even neater. For example, within a "Project X" section, you can have subsections like "Research," "Planning," "Execution," etc.
- **Order of sections**: You can rearrange the order of sections by simply dragging and dropping. This allows you to adapt the layout of your notebook as your project evolves.

Managing pages and subpages

Pages are where the actual notes are taken in OneNote. A page can contain text, images, tables, links, or file attachments. However, to maximize the effectiveness of your pages, OneNote allows you to manage them in an advanced way through **subpages and** formatting tools.

- **Creating subpages**: If a page becomes too long or complex, you can create **subpages** to further subdivide the content. For example, suppose you have a home page for a meeting. In that case, you can create subpages for specific topics discussed during the conference.
- **Hierarchical organization**: Subpages can be used to create a logical content hierarchy. This is useful when taking notes on complex projects requiring detailed information organization.
- **Page order**: You can quickly reorder pages by dragging and dropping them to fit the organization of information into your workflow. You can also create hyperlinks between pages to quickly switch between topics.

Quick Notes and Audio Recordings

OneNote 2025 introduces further improvements in the management of **quick notes** and **audio recordings**, essential tools for those who work in fast-paced environments or need to quickly capture information without worrying too much about formatting.

- **Quick Notes**: This feature allows you to take quick notes in a **Quick Notes** window that can be easily recalled during meetings or brainstorming. You can then organize your quick notes later in the appropriate notebook.
- **Audio** recordings: If you prefer to record voice notes, OneNote allows you to **record audio directly** within pages. This feature is handy during meetings or lectures when you need to review discussion details later. You can also sync recordings with your notes, allowing you to listen back to specific moments from the recording as you scroll through your notes.

Integration with Power Automate for automation

A significant aspect of OneNote 2025 is the integration with **Microsoft Power Automate**, which allows you to automate various tasks within the application. With Power Automate, you can set up workflows that automatically trigger in response to specific events or actions within OneNote.

Some examples of automation include:

- **Automatic creation of new pages**: You can set up a workflow that automatically creates a new page in OneNote whenever you receive a specific email or whenever a meeting is scheduled in Outlook.
- **Automatic archiving of notes**: You can create a workflow that automatically archives completed notes in a specific OneDrive or SharePoint folder.

Automatic reminders: Thanks to the integration with To-Do and Planner, you can automate the creation of reminders and tasks based on the content of your notes.

Integration with Outlook and other applications

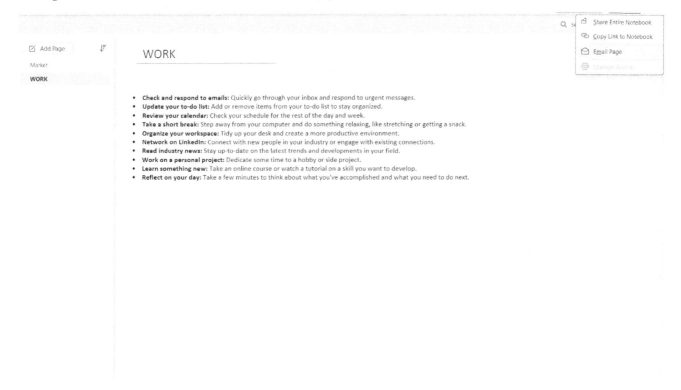

One feature that makes **Microsoft OneNote 2025** particularly powerful is its deep **integration with the other applications in the Microsoft 365 suite**, especially **Outlook, Teams,** and **SharePoint**. These integrations simplify information management and significantly improve collaboration between team members by allowing data to be centralized and connected between applications without switching between programs. In this paragraph, we'll explore how to make the most of these integrations to make your workflow and collaboration more seamless.

Outlook Integration: Notes and Meetings

The integration between **OneNote** and **Outlook is** one of the most useful aspects for those who use these applications daily, especially for managing meetings, emails, and tasks.
OneNote integrates seamlessly with your Outlook calendar, allowing you to take notes directly within a scheduled meeting. When you create or join a meeting in Outlook, you can open a new notebook in OneNote to automatically link your notes to your calendar event. This lets you keep all meeting information centralized, including attendees, agenda, and topics discussed.

Here's how to use this feature:
- Click on a meeting in your Outlook calendar and select **Meeting Notes**.
- Choose whether to take notes just for you or share the notebook with participants.
- Your notes will be automatically linked to the Outlook event, making it easy to access all relevant information quickly.

- **Linked emails and notes**: With OneNote, you can link your emails directly to your notes, making it easier to keep track of conversations or information received via email. If you have an email containing important project details, you can send it directly to OneNote as a notes page. This way, critical information is saved and organized within your notebook without searching through emails.

You can easily do it like this:
- In Outlook, select an email and click **Send to OneNote**.
- Choose the notebook or section where you want to store the email.
- OneNote will create a new page with the email's content while keeping the link to the original email in Outlook for easy reference.

Microsoft Teams Integration: Collaboration and Sharing

Integration with **Microsoft Teams** benefits teams that work on shared projects or need to collaborate regularly. OneNote can be integrated into Teams in several ways to improve **real-time collaboration**.
You can add a OneNote laptop directly to a Teams channel, making it easy for team members to collaborate on the same notes. Each team member can access, edit, and contribute information to the notebook, all within the Teams interface. This is useful for meetings, brainstorming, or project management, where multiple people must work on the same documents.

To add OneNote to a channel in Teams:
- Within a channel, click **Add a card** (+).
- Select **OneNote** and choose the notebook you want to share or create a new one.
- Team members can now collaborate directly in the notebook without leaving Teams.

During a meeting in Teams, you can use OneNote to take notes in real time real-time and share them with all participants. Notes will be visible to everyone and updated in real time, making collaborating easier during virtual meetings.

SharePoint Integration: Document Storage and Management

SharePoint is a powerful tool for document management and centralized information storage. When you use OneNote in conjunction with SharePoint, you can store your notebooks in a SharePoint **document library**, ensuring that everyone on your team has access to the information they need and that your documents are well organized.
- **Centralized storage of notebooks**: You can save OneNote notebooks to a SharePoint document library, ensuring all team members have access to archived notes and projects. This also allows you to use SharePoint's advanced security features to protect your documents and manage access permissions.
- **Permission management**: With SharePoint, you can manage access **permissions** to your notebooks in detail. You can decide who can view, edit, or manage content, ensuring that only

authorized people can access certain information. This feature is handy when working on sensitive projects or with external collaborators.

Automation and integration with Power Automate

Another valuable tool for those who use OneNote in an advanced way is **Power Automate**. This tool allows you to automate a series of operations within OneNote and integrate it with other applications in the Microsoft suite and beyond. For example, you can set up workflows that automate the creation of new notes, the organization of notebooks, or the sending of notifications.

Some examples of automation include:

- **Automate the creation of new notes**: You can configure Power Automate to automatically create a new page in OneNote when an event is added to your Outlook calendar, ensuring that your meeting notes are always ready.
- **To-Do and Planner integration**: When you create a to-do list in OneNote, you can set up a workflow that automatically transfers tasks to Microsoft **To-Do** or **Planner**, resulting in a detailed work plan that's synchronized across applications.

Advanced Tips

Microsoft OneNote 2025 is more than just a note-taking tool: it's a control center for organizing information efficiently and productively. This section is dedicated to exploring **advanced techniques** to unlock OneNote's full potential, improving your ability to manage workflow, optimize the organization of your notes, and collaborate more effectively. These tips will help you **maximize productivity** and stay on top of everything.

Using Page Templates to Standardize Notes

One of the most valuable features for organizing your work is using **page templates** in OneNote. These templates allow you to maintain a consistent structure across your notes, saving time when you need to manage information similarly or repetitively.

- **Pre-built templates**: OneNote offers several templates for meeting notes, checklists, agendas, and project plans. These templates have ready-made fields to quickly fill in to keep your notes neat.
- **Creating custom templates**: If you need a specific format for your work, you can make a **template** in OneNote. This allows you to include fixed fields for goals, dates, task assignments, and other information you must have available frequently.
- **Quick application of templates**: You can apply a template to any new page, ensuring that every time you create a new note, the structure is already ready to use. This is especially useful for recurring meetings or reports that need to follow consistent formatting.

Visual organization with the use of labels and colors

Another powerful tool for organizing and retrieving information quickly in OneNote is **labels** and **colors**. Labels allow you to assign specific categories to paragraphs or items within your notes, making it easier to search and filter information later.

- **Assign labels**: OneNote offers a variety of **default labels**, such as "To-Do," "Important," "Question," or "Idea." You can also create custom labels to suit your needs, allowing you to categorize and organize notes according to specific criteria.
- **Label-based search**: You can use OneNote's search feature for specific labels throughout your notebook. For example, you can search for all tasks marked as "To-Do" or all-important information labeled as "Important."
- **Using colors for sections and pages**: A simple yet effective way to visually organize information is to distinguish sections or pages within your notebook. This allows you to quickly identify different areas of your laptop without reading each title or subheading.

Create hyperlinks between pages

An advanced feature of OneNote that can improve work organization is the ability to create **hyperlinks between** pages and sections. This feature links related information within the same notebook, making navigating and consulting content easier.

- **Creating links between pages**: You can make a link from one page to another within the same notebook or different notebooks. For example, one section contains a project summary, and another contains detailed notes. In that case, you can link the two pages to easily switch between them.
- **Use external links**: In addition to linking pages within OneNote, you can also insert hyperlinks to external resources such as documents on SharePoint, websites, or files stored in OneDrive. This makes OneNote a true hub for all relevant project resources.

Take advantage of OneNote's advanced search

The **search** function in OneNote 2025 is potent. It allows you to find information in seconds, even within huge and complex notebooks. You can search for keywords, phrases, labels, and even content found in images or audio recordings.

- **Search for text in pictures**: With optical character recognition (OCR), OneNote can search for and identify text in pictures. If you have entered a scan of a document or a photo with text, you can use the search function to find the text in that image.
- **Search in audio recordings**: If you use OneNote to record voice notes during meetings or lectures, you can search for specific words within the tapes. OneNote recognizes the words spoken in the audio file, making it easy to find critical points without listening to the entire recording again.
- **Search by labels**: You can also narrow your search to specific labels. For example, if you only want to find notes marked as "Important," just enter the filter in the search bar to see relevant results immediately.

Use OneNote for project management

OneNote is perfect for **project management**, allowing you to collect, organize, and update your project information in one place. You can manage each project phase using sections and pages to track progress, prioritize, and record the details of each meeting or review.

- **Checklists and tasks**: Use **checklists** to manage tasks and activities within the project. At the beginning of the project, create a task list and update completed tasks with the "To-Do" feature.
- **Integration with Planner and To-Do**: With OneNote's integration with Microsoft **Planner** and **To-Do**, you can directly link tasks from your notebook to task management tools. This allows a clear view of what must be done and who is responsible for improving time and resource management.

Automate repetitive tasks with Power Automate

As discussed in the previous paragraph, **Power Automate** is an advanced tool that allows you to **automate** various tasks within OneNote, improving efficiency and reducing the time it takes to handle repetitive tasks. For example, you can set up a workflow that automatically creates a new note whenever you receive an email on a topic or join a meeting.

Integration with other tools: You can also integrate Power Automate with different project management tools, such as Microsoft Planner, to automate the transfer of tasks from OneNote to Planner or Outlook.

9. Microsoft Access 2025

Microsoft Access 2025 is one of the most complete and powerful tools for **managing and building databases**. It is designed for professionals who want to organize and analyze data efficiently. Access allows you to create customized and flexible solutions, whether you need to manage large amounts of data or create complex reports. This chapter will focus on how to use Access to create and manage databases, analyze data with advanced queries, and automate processes using built-in tools such as **macros**.

Access is particularly useful in business or academic environments, where data analysis and information management must be precise and well-structured. By integrating with other **Microsoft 365 applications**, Access becomes a critical element in a workflow where data, reporting, and automation play a central role. This chapter will guide you through the essential features, passing through advanced data analysis and building complex databases.

Introduction to Microsoft Access

Microsoft Access 2025 is relational database management software that allows users to efficiently create, manage, and analyze **structured data**. Unlike spreadsheets like Excel, Access is designed specifically for managing **large volumes of data** and allowing users to create custom systems that can handle complex information in a scalable and flexible way.

One of the main advantages of Access is its ability to **link information between different tables** using the power of relational **databases**. This means you can store data in separate tables and establish relationships between them, thus avoiding duplication and making information management more efficient. For example, if you manage a customer database, you can have one table for customers' personal information, another for orders placed, and another for payment details. With **table relationships**, Access lets you connect this data and create reports or extracts that combine information from multiple sources. Access stands out for its ability to adapt to various uses, from managing small individual projects to building complex enterprise databases. Whether you need to manage data for a small shop, a school, or a large corporation, Access gives you a powerful and versatile platform to build systems tailored to your needs.

A user-friendly interface and powerful tools

Despite its power, **Microsoft Access 2025 is** designed with a user-friendly interface, allowing even novice users to start working with databases efficiently. The ribbon is like Microsoft 365 applications like Word and Excel. It provides quick access to the most used tools, such as creating tables, queries, forms, and reports. Access also offers advanced tools that allow you **to write SQL code**, create **custom macros,** and integrate Access with other applications using **VBA (Visual Basic for Applications) for those who need even more granular control.** Access is suitable for those who want simple data management and need to develop more complex solutions.

Relational Data Management

One of Microsoft Access's strengths is its ability to manage **relational databases**. This type of database organizes data into tables connected to each other through primary keys and relationships. This approach avoids data redundancy, reducing the chance of errors and improving efficiency.
In Access, you can create tables to store data and then define relationships between them, such as linking a customer table to an order table. This lets you query and update customer and order information simultaneously, ensuring your data is consistent and up to date.

Create custom applications

Another significant advantage of Access is the ability to create real **custom applications**. Using tools such as **forms**, **queries,** and **reports**, users can build custom user interfaces and solutions that make it easier to manage and query data without writing complex code.

- **Forms**: Forms in Access allow you to create graphical interfaces that make entering and updating data simple and intuitive. You can customize forms to fit your needs, including fields, buttons, and other controls that allow you to perform operations directly on the database.
- **Queries**: Queries allow you to extract, filter, and sort data based on specific criteria. Access allows you to create complex queries with multiple conditions to get the necessary information, making your data analysis faster.
- **Reports**: Reports allow you to present data in a structured and professional way, making it easy to create printable documents to share with colleagues or clients.

Integration with other Microsoft applications

Access is seamlessly integrated with other **Microsoft 365 applications**, such as **Excel, Outlook,** and **SharePoint**, making it easy to import and export data. You can connect Access databases with Excel spreadsheets, send reports directly through Outlook, or store databases in SharePoint for centralized and secure access.

- **Excel integration**: Many users start working with data using Excel and then switch to Access when the data becomes too large or complex. Excel integration allows you to import spreadsheets directly into Access, where you can manage data more efficiently.
- **SharePoint integration**: With SharePoint, you can share Access databases with other users and allow them to access data from anywhere while maintaining control over security and access permissions.

Creating and managing databases

Creating **and managing databases** in **Microsoft Access 2025** is one of the fundamental operations for organizing and maintaining data in a structured and easily accessible way. Access allows you to create relational databases that link tables together, eliminating redundancies and improving data consistency. This paragraph will explore the basics of creating a database, managing tables, the importance of data normalization, and some techniques for keeping your database efficient and tidy.

Creating a new database

When you start a new project in **Microsoft Access**, the first thing you need to do is create a new database. This can be done in a few simple steps using Access' pre-built templates or starting from a blank database to customize every aspect of the project.

- **Creating an empty database**: Creating a new one allows you to start from scratch, building your tables, queries, forms, and reports according to your needs. This approach is helpful for specific projects that require a wholly customized structure.
    - Go to the Access home screen and select **New Blank Database**.
    - Give your database a name and choose where you want to save it (usually on OneDrive or a local drive).
    - Once created, Access will take you to the design interface, where you can start building the tables.
- **Use pre-built templates**: If you don't want to start from scratch, Access provides several **templates** for common databases, such as inventory, customer, or project management. These templates already include pre-built tables, queries, and reports, which you can customize to suit your needs.
    - On the home screen, select a **pre-made template** from the available templates.
    - The database will be created with a ready-made structure, which you can modify and expand according to the needs of your project.

Table management

Tables are the heart of every database. In Access, tables store data in rows (records) and columns (fields). Each table should be carefully designed to ensure that the data is organized efficiently and that relevant information is easily retrieved.

Once the database is created, the next step is to create a table to house the data. Each table must have at least one key column (called a **primary key**), which uniquely identifies each record. This ensures that data is not duplicated and that every information can be easily found and updated.

- Go to **Create > Table** and start defining the table's fields (columns). Each field must have a **name** and data **type** (e.g., text, numeric, date, etc.).
- After you create the fields, set one of them as **the primary key** (often the record's unique ID).

When creating a table, choosing the appropriate data types for each field is essential. This helps avoid input errors and improves the efficiency of queries and reports. For example, fields that contain numbers should be defined as **numeric,** while those that contain text should be defined as **textual.** You can also apply validation rules to ensure that the data you enter is correct (for example, by mandating that the "Date" field contains only valid dates).

Data Normalization

Normalization is organizing data within a database to reduce redundancy and improve data integrity. A well-normalized database allows information to be linked logically. It ensures that each piece of data is stored only once, reducing the risk of errors and duplication.

- **Avoid data duplication**: The same data can be repeated across multiple tables in an unnormalized database. For example, a customer's name might appear in the "Customers" table and the "Orders" table. Normalization eliminates this duplication by only storing the customer's name in the "Customers" table and linking the "Orders" table with a **foreign key**.
- **Multi-table structure**: Normalization involves splitting data into multiple tables, each containing only the information directly relevant to a specific topic. The tables are then connected through **relationships**, which allow you to access the data dynamically without duplication.

Relationships between tables

One of Microsoft Access's key features is the ability to create **relationships** between tables. This allows you to connect data between different tables using primary and foreign keys, improving database organization and making it easier to run queries and reports.

- **Types of relationships**: Table relationships can be **one-to-one, one-to-many,** or **many-to-many**. The kind of relationship you use depends on the nature of the data you're managing. For example, a customer may have many orders in a one-to-many relationship. Still, each order is associated with only one customer.
- **Referential integrity**: When creating relationships, you can set **referential integrity** rules to ensure that your data is always consistent. For example, Access will not allow you to delete a customer if orders are associated with that customer unless these orders are updated or deleted accordingly.

Data maintenance and updating

Once you have created your database and set up the relationships between the tables, managing and updating your data is crucial. Access provides tools to simplify this process, such as the ability **to import data** from other sources (such as Excel) and create input **masks** to make it easier to insert new records.

- **Input masks**: Forms in Access allow you to create simple and intuitive interfaces for entering data. You can customize forms with buttons, drop-down lists, and other controls to simplify data input and reduce the risk of errors.
- **Importing data**: If you already have existing data in other formats, such as Excel or CSV, Access allows you to **import it directly** into the database, eliminating the need to manually enter each record. You can also link external data to automatically update the database whenever the original data changes.

Data analysis with advanced queries

One of the most powerful aspects of **Microsoft Access 2025** is its ability to perform **advanced data analysis** using queries. Queries are the primary tool for querying the database to extract, sort, and filter data based on specific criteria. This paragraph will explore the various types of queries you can create in Access and how to use them to gain insights from your data. We'll dive deeper into **select, parametric**, and **append queries** to update or modify data and more advanced queries to perform complex analysis.

Select Query

Select **queries** are the most common type of Query in Access. They allow you to view, filter, and sort data from one or more tables. These queries are essential for extracting specific information without changing the original data in the database.

When you create a select query, you can choose which fields to display and apply criteria to filter the data. For example, you can make a query that shows all customers who have placed an order in the last 30 days or who filter products by a specific price range.

- Go to **Create > Query Structure** and select the tables or queries from which you want to extract data.
- Add the fields you want to display in the grid and apply filter criteria (for example, show only records with an order date after a specific date).
- Run the Query to see the filtered results.

Besides filtering data, you can use select queries to **sort** results based on one or more fields. For example, you can sort records by date, customer name, or number of orders. You can also **group** the results to get totals, sums, or counts. This is useful when you want to see how many sales each seller has made or how many orders have been received for each product.

Parametric queries

Parametric queries provide additional flexibility by requiring users to enter parameters when the Query is executed. In other words, instead of specifying a fixed criterion, you can ask the user to enter a value for the filter each time the Query is executed.

- **Example of a parametric query**: If you want to display orders placed on a specific date, you can create a query that asks the user to enter the date at the time of execution. Access will only show records that match that date.
  - In the query creation grid, instead of entering a fixed criterion, write **[Enter order date] in the** date field.
  - When you run the Query, Access will open a window where the user can enter the desired date. The results will only show orders placed on that date.
- **Advantages of parametric queries**: This Query type is beneficial for dynamic reports, where the selection criteria must be changed frequently without recreating or modifying the Query each time.

Append and Update Queries

In addition to extracting data, Access also allows you to use queries to **modify** or **update** the database data. Append and **update queries** are two types of queries that will enable you to modify existing records or add new data from another source.

- **Append queries**: This allows you to **add new records** to a table from another table or data source. For example, suppose you have a database with new orders received through an external system. In that case, you can use an append query to automatically add these orders to the central Access database.

- You create a query that selects the records you want to append and then adds them to a specified target table.
- **Update queries**: Update queries allow you to **modify data** based on specific criteria. This is useful if you need to update many records simultaneously. For example, if you need to increase the prices of a product group by 10%, you can create an update query that changes the price field based on the criteria you choose.

Table Creation Query

Table **creation queries** copy data from one or more tables to a **new table**. This feature is useful when you need to store or copy data for use in another context without altering the structure of the original tables. This type of Query can store old records or create a simplified table version for use in a specific report.

- In the query creation grid, select the fields you want to copy to the new table and specify the name of the target table. When you run the query, Access will create a query table with the selected data.

Merge queries and cross-queries

Merge **queries** and **cross-queries are** advanced tools that allow you to combine or compare data from multiple tables in specific ways.

- Merge queries combine data from multiple tables into a single query. For example, suppose you have a table that contains customer orders and another table with returns. In that case, you can merge the data to get an overview of all order-related movements.
- **Cross-queries**: Cross-queries allow you **to summarize data** in a pivot-like table, which is helpful for compactly visualizing aggregated information. For example, you can use a cross-query to see the total sales for each product, broken down by month.

Query optimization

When working with large databases, queries can become slow if not optimized properly. To improve performance, it's essential to:

- **Use indexes**: Applying indexes to frequently used fields in search and filter queries can significantly improve response times.
- **Avoid unnecessary fields**: When creating a query, select only the fields needed for the report or analysis, reducing the load on the system.

Use nested queries with caution: Nested queries, which use other queries as sources, can become complex and slow. Try to limit their use to cases where they are really needed.

Advanced database construction

In the world of data management, the ability to build **advanced databases** is critical to structuring, organizing, and connecting large amounts of information efficiently. **Microsoft Access 2025** provides powerful tools to create complex databases, with advanced features such as **relationships between tables**, **primary and secondary keys**, and **indexes** to optimize performance. This section will explore the techniques for building advanced databases, from creating relational tables to managing data with referential integrity.

Creating Relational Tables

At the heart of any advanced database is the organization of data into **relational tables**. A relational table allows you to logically link information across multiple tables, eliminating data redundancy and improving information consistency. Access enables you to create tables that share common data using **primary keys** and **foreign keys**.

- **Primary key**: Every table in a relational database must have a **primary key**. This field uniquely identifies each record within the table. For example, in the "Customers" table, the primary key might be the "Customer ID" field, a unique number assigned to each customer.
- **Foreign key**: Foreign **keys** are used to create links between tables. For example, in the "Orders" table, the "Customer ID" field might be a foreign key that links to the "Customers" table. This allows you to associate each order with a specific customer without duplicating customer information in each order.

Setting up table relationships

One key feature of a relational database is the ability to **establish relationships** between tables, connecting data logically and consistently. In Access, you can define three main types of relationships: **one-to-one**, **one-to-many**, and **many-to-many**.

- **One-to-many relationship**: This type of relationship is the most common in a database. It means that one record in one table can be linked to many records in another table. For example, a customer may have many orders, but each is associated with only one customer. This relationship is created by linking a primary key in one table to a foreign key in another table.
- **Many-to-many relationship**: To implement a many-to-many relationship, you must use a **junction table**. This type of relationship occurs when many records in one table can be linked to many records in another table. For example, an order might contain many products, and each product can be associated with many orders. The splice table handles these complex relationships, allowing you to maintain data integrity.

Referential integrity and validation rules

Implementing referential integrity is critical to ensuring data consistency and correctness in a relational database. Referential integrity is based on rules that ensure relationships between tables are maintained and that data is consistent.

- **Setting referential integrity**: In Access, you can configure referential integrity when you create or edit a relationship between two tables. This ensures that, for example, you can't delete a customer from the "Customers" table if there are orders associated with that customer in the "Orders" table unless those orders are handled correctly.
- **Cascading update and delete**: Access offers **cascading update** and **cascading delete** options, which automate the update or deletion of linked data. For example, suppose you change a record in the "Customers" table. In that case, Access can automatically update all related documents in the "Orders" table. Similarly, Access can automatically delete the associated orders if you delete a customer, ensuring no orphaned data remains.

Performance Optimization with the Use of Indexes

When working with large databases, optimizing performance is critical **to** ensure that queries and data access operations are fast and efficient. One way to improve access performance is to use **indexes**.

- **Indexes on key fields**: Indexes are often applied to primary and foreign keys to speed up search and sorting operations. Access can retrieve data faster when a field is indexed, as it doesn't have to scroll through the entire database to find the required information.
- **Using multiple indexes**: Besides indexing primary keys, you can index fields frequently used in queries. For example, if you often run queries based on the "Order Date" field, it's helpful to create an index for that field to improve performance.

However, it is essential to use indexes carefully, as excessive use can slow down data ingestion and update operations.

Transaction Management and Rollback

Another advanced feature of Microsoft Access is managing transactions and ensuring data operations are performed securely. Transactions allow you to perform a series of database operations in a single block, ensuring that all operations are completed are completed successfully or not applied (this technique is called **rollback**).

- **Transactions**: When you perform a transaction, Access allows you to make various changes to the database, such as inserting new records, updating data, or deleting information. Suppose something goes wrong during the operation (for example, a system error or an unexpected condition). In that case, you can cancel the entire transaction, restoring the database to its previous state.
- **Rollback**: Rollback is a feature that allows you to cancel a partial transaction in case of an error. This ensures that the database remains consistent and that no changes are applied until all operations are completed.

Database Backup and Restore

To protect your data and ensure that the database is always secure, it is essential to make regular **backups** and know how to restore the database in the event of data loss or corruption.

- **Regular backups**: Access offers tools to create backup copies of your database, which allow you to save the current state of your data and restore it if necessary. Making frequent backups is a good practice, especially before making significant changes to the database structure or data.
- **Data recovery**: In the event of a failure or data loss, restoring from a backup allows you to revert to a previous database version, minimizing the risk of disruption and ensuring business continuity.

Process automation with macros

In **Microsoft Access 2025**, macros are a powerful tool for automating repetitive tasks and improving the efficiency of your daily work. Macros can perform various predefined operations in the database, reducing the risk of errors and speeding up manual tasks. In this paragraph, we'll explore how to create, manage, and customize macros in Access while integrating with other Microsoft 365 tools to create automated workflows.

What are macros in Microsoft Access?

Macros in Access are commands that run automatically based on certain conditions or actions. They're a "mini programming" that allows you to automate tasks without writing VBA (Visual Basic for Applications) code. However, advanced macros can interact with VBA for even more customization.

Macros are handy for:

- **Automate repetitive tasks**: For example, you can create a macro that executes a series of queries each time it is launched or opens and closes specific modules based on certain conditions.

- **Take actions in response to events**: You can link a macro to an event, such as opening a form or updating a field, so that Access automatically performs a series of actions whenever that event occurs.
- **Manage complex processes**: Macros can automate processes that require multiple tables, forms, and queries to interact, making your workflow easier.

Creating a Macro in Access

Thanks to the software's user-friendly interface, creating a macro in Microsoft Access is relatively simple. You don't need to know code to start working with macros. Access provides a design grid that lets you select predefined actions to perform in response to specific events.

Steps to create a macro:
1. Go to **Create > Macro** in the ribbon.
2. Access will open a designer where you can choose from a list of **actions** (such as opening a form, running a query, appending data, etc.).
3. Select the desired actions and set the parameters. For example, you can configure the macro to run a query and then open a report that displays the results.
4. Save the macro and link the execution to an event (such as opening a form or clicking a button).

Macro example: If you manage an order database, you can create a macro that, once a new order is received, performs a series of actions: queues the new order in a table, updates the inventory and sends a summary report via email.

Types of Macros in Access

Access offers several types of macros, each with a specific purpose and different levels of complexity.
- **Action Macros** are the simplest macros and perform a variety of sequential actions. They can automate tasks such as opening forms, running queries, printing reports, or updating records.
- **Built-in macros**: These macros are inserted directly into the events of forms or controls. For example, you can link a built-in macro to the "Save" button in a form so that a series of actions are performed each time the user clicks the button.
- **Data macros**: Data macros are a new feature over previous versions of Access and allow you to perform operations directly on data, like triggers in SQL databases. These macros can be configured to perform actions whenever a record is inserted, updated, or deleted.

Automate workflows with macros

One of the most potent uses of macros is to automate **complex workflows**. You can configure Access to perform a series of operations sequentially without manual intervention, improving efficiency and reducing the risk of errors.

- **Multiple query execution**: A macro can run various queries sequentially. For example, run a query that selects new orders, then an inventory status update, and finally, a query that generates a report on updated data.
- **Interaction with forms and reports**: Macros can automatically open forms or reports, depending on the user's actions. For example, when the user completes a form, a macro can be configured to save the data, close the form, and open a report that displays the data entered.

Macro integration with other Microsoft applications

Another great feature of Access is its **integration with other Microsoft 365 applications**, such as **Excel, Outlook, Word,** and **Power Automate**. Macros can be configured to interact with these applications and create automated workflows that involve multiple tools.
- **Outlook integration**: You can create a macro that automatically sends an email through Outlook when a specific event occurs in the database, such as completing an order or reaching an inventory threshold.
- **Excel integration**: Access allows you to automatically export data to Excel using macros, making it easy to analyze or create advanced spreadsheet reports.
- **Automate with Power Automate**: With **Power Automate**, you can integrate Access into more complex business workflows. For example, you can set up a flow that automatically updates an Excel sheet whenever a new record is entered in Access, creates a task in Planner, or sends a notification in Teams.

Use of advanced macros and interaction with VBA

If you need a higher level of customization, you can combine macros with **Visual** Basic for Applications (VBA) code. Macros offer quick and easy automation, but VBA allows you to write **custom code** to perform even more complex actions.
- **When to use VBA**: If your macro requires more complex conditional logic or needs to interact with other external applications or systems, you may prefer to use VBA. For example, if you want to create a workflow that performs different actions based on a condition (e.g., if the order exceeds a certain threshold, notify a supervisor; otherwise, update the order status), VBA is the best choice.
- **Integration between macros and VBA**: You can start with a macro to handle basic operations and then extend its functionality using VBA. Access lets you intuitively switch between the macro window and VBA programming.

Data Backup and Protection

One of the most critical aspects of managing a database is ensuring its security and integrity. **Microsoft Access 2025** offers several tools to make **regular backups** and protect your database from errors, corruption, or data loss. This paragraph will explore techniques for performing backups, restoring the database, and taking security measures to protect sensitive information.

Importance of Regular Backup

A database contains crucial data, both for day-to-day business and long-term management. Without regular backups, a hardware failure, human error, or virus can cause the irreversible loss of information. Making **periodic backups** is a critical preventative measure to minimize the risk of losing valuable data.

- **Automatic backup**: In Microsoft Access, you can set up automatic backups or perform a backup whenever you make significant changes to the database structure or data. Regular backup ensures you can revert to a previous version of the database in case of a problem, reducing the risk of operational disruptions.
- **Backup frequency**: How often you back up depends on your database usage. We recommend daily backups for frequently used databases or were data changes daily. For less-used databases, weekly or monthly backups may be sufficient.

How to make a backup in Access

Microsoft Access offers a simple process for taking database backups. When you make a backup, you save a full copy of the database file, which you can restore if necessary. Here's how to back up your database:

Steps to backup:
1. Open the database you want to back up.
2. Go to **File> Save As > Database Backup**.
3. Choose a safe location (preferably an external or cloud drive) to save the backup and rename the File to indicate the date and time of the backup.
4. Click **Save**. Access will create a complete copy of the database in its current state.

When you save the backup file, it will be an exact replica of the original database, including all data, tables, queries, macros, and forms.

Database Restore

If the original database fails or becomes corrupted, you can quickly **restore** it using the backup file. Restore is one of the most essential functions, as it allows you to restore the database to a previous state without losing critical information.

Steps to restore a backup:
1. Locate the backup file you created earlier.
2. Close any current version of the database you're using.
3. Copy the backup file to the original location or a new location if you prefer to keep it separate from the corrupted File.
4. Open the backup file with Microsoft Access. The database will be restored to its exact state after the backup.

Making frequent backups ensures that you can restore the database and quickly resume operations without significant data loss, even in the event of failures or errors.

Password protection of the database

To ensure the security of your data, especially in shared environments or databases accessible by multiple users, it is essential **to protect the database with a password**. Microsoft Access encrypts the database file and requires a password to access it.

Setting the password:
1. Open the database you want to protect.
2. Go to **File> Info > Encrypt with Password**.
3. Enter and confirm your desired password. Ensure your password is strong and secure, as Access uses encryption to protect your data.
4. Click **OK.** From now on, anyone who tries to open the database must enter the password to access it.

Password protection is essential for protecting data from unauthorized access, mainly when the database contains sensitive information or is used in a multi-user environment.

In a business context, it is common for an Access database to be shared among multiple users, each with different levels of responsibility and need for access to the data. To ensure security, Access allows you **to manage permissions** and restrict access to certain parts of the database.

- **Access control**: You can configure Access to manage who can view, modify, or delete data within the database. For example, you might only allow certain users to access specific tables or queries. In contrast, others may only have access to reports.
- **Permission management**: Permission management is crucial to prevent unauthorized users from modifying or deleting critical data. Access provides user management tools that allow you to set specific roles and assign permissions based on your organization's needs.

Saving the database to the cloud

Another vital measure to protect your data is to ensure your database is **stored securely**. In addition to performing local backups, you can save your database to a cloud platform, such as **OneDrive** or **SharePoint**, to ensure that your data is always accessible and secure, even in the event of local hardware failures.

- **Save to OneDrive**: Saving your database to OneDrive allows you to access it from any device and ensures that a secure copy is always available online.
- **SharePoint integration**: Access easily integrates with **SharePoint**, allowing you to share your database and collaborate on data in real-time. SharePoint also offers centralized permission management and advanced security, reducing the risk of unauthorized access or data loss.

Finally, it is essential to monitor database activity to ensure that no unwanted actions compromise the integrity of the data. Access provides tools to **monitor changes** and **log user activity**, helping you quickly identify errors or suspicious behavior.

- **Change auditing**: Using audit features, you can track who changed a record, what changes were made, and when they were made. This is especially useful for shared databases, where it is essential to track changes to avoid errors or unauthorized manipulation.

Error notifications: You can configure Access to send error notifications or logs when issues occur while running a query or macro, allowing you to act promptly.

10. Microsoft OneDrive 2025

Microsoft OneDrive 2025 is an essential cloud storage tool for anyone who wants to access their files from any device while ensuring security and ease of use. Its ability to **sync and share files** makes it ideal for individuals and teams working on collaborative projects. With the growing need to access documents, images, and other files from anywhere, OneDrive allows you to centralize all your data in one secure, always up-to-date platform.

In this chapter, we'll explore the critical features of **OneDrive 2025**, including **secure file syncing**, organizing for collaborative projects, and a range of **practical file management tips**, including automated backup and sync processes. We'll look at how OneDrive simplifies day-to-day document management and improves collaboration and efficiency, especially in hybrid or remote work environments.

Get started with OneDrive.

Microsoft OneDrive 2025 is Microsoft's cloud solution for storing, syncing, and sharing files. Designed for individuals and teams, OneDrive allows you to access your documents from any device anytime while providing security and flexibility. With an intuitive interface and seamless integration with other **Microsoft 365** applications, OneDrive has established itself as a fundamental tool for managing files in personal and professional settings.

Sync and share files securely

One of the main functions of OneDrive is the ability to **sync files** across multiple devices. Any changes you make to a file on one device are immediately updated and reflected on other devices linked to the same account. For example, you edit a Word document on your computer. In that case, you can continue working on it later from your smartphone without manually transferring the file or worrying about duplicates.

The synchronization process is fully automated: OneDrive works in the background to keep all your files updated, eliminating the need for manual saves or transfers. With real-time syncing, OneDrive ensures that you always have fast and reliable access to the latest files, no matter your device.

In addition, OneDrive offers advanced options for **secure file sharing**. You can share individual documents or folders with others, setting read or edit permissions as needed. For example, you can allow your collaborators to edit a document. At the same time, you can only grant your customers or partners read access. Your files are protected by **advanced security features**, such as password protection or the ability to set an expiration date for shared links, to ensure that access is temporary and controlled.

File organization for collaborative projects

OneDrive is a storage tool and a powerful means of managing collaborative projects. Thanks to the creation of **dedicated folders**, organizing files by project is easy. These folders can be shared with work teams, making accessing all the documents needed for a specific project easy.

A beneficial aspect of collaboration is the ability to work on shared documents simultaneously. With the **co-authorship** feature, multiple people can edit the same document in real-time and view other users' edits live. This eliminates the need to send various document versions via email, reducing confusion and duplicates. Collaboration on shared files benefits distributed teams, who can work on the same documents regardless of their geographic location.

Another essential feature is document **versioning**. Whenever a file is changed, OneDrive automatically saves a new version. If necessary, you can always return to a previous version of the file, recovering lost information or correcting errors made during editing. This feature is helpful for both individuals and teams, providing additional **security** in case a document is changed incorrectly or accidentally.

File management tips

In this paragraph, we'll explore some **practical tips** for using **Microsoft OneDrive 2025** in file management, focusing on **automating backup processes** and **syncing data**. OneDrive is a flexible and powerful tool that, when used correctly, can significantly simplify the organization and protection of your documents.

Automation of backup and synchronization processes

One of the critical benefits of OneDrive is the ability to **automate file backup and synchronization**, reducing the need to manually manage documents and minimizing the risk of data loss. Using these features in the best way saves time and ensures the security of your files, which will always be up-to-date and available on all your devices.

OneDrive automatically syncs files between the devices linked to your account. Once configured, the service will sync in the background, ensuring that any changes made on one device are replicated to the others. This feature is handy for those who use multiple devices (e.g., a laptop at work and a smartphone on the go), allowing you to always access the most up-to-date version of a document without the need for manual transfers.

To turn on automatic syncing, link the folders you want to OneDrive. For example, you can sync your computer's "Documents" folder so that all the files it contains are automatically saved to OneDrive and accessed from other devices.

Automatic Backup

OneDrive offers the ability to configure **automatic Backup** of critical folders, such as Documents, Pictures, and Desktop, ensuring that essential data is always saved in the cloud. This process happens without manual intervention: once set up, OneDrive regularly performs automatic backups, ensuring that your files are protected from hardware failure or accidental deletion.

To turn on automatic Backup, follow these steps:
- Go to OneDrive settings and select **Backup> Manage backups**.
- Choose the folders you want to include in the automatic Backup.
- Confirm and start syncing. From now on, every file saved in the selected folders will be automatically copied to OneDrive.

File Recovery

In addition to Backup, OneDrive offers advanced tools for **restoring files** in case of errors or accidental deletions. If a file is deleted by mistake, you can quickly recover it from the **OneDrive Recycle Bin**, which keeps a copy of deleted files for a set time (up to 30 days for personal accounts or longer for business accounts).

Plus, with the **version history feature**, you can recover previous versions of a file in case of unwanted changes. This is especially useful when working on collaborative projects, where multiple users can edit the same document. You can return to a previous version with just a few clicks and undo any unwanted errors or changes.

Selective Sync

OneDrive lets you manage storage space on devices with **selective sync**. This feature lets you choose which files and folders to sync locally to your device and which ones to keep only in the cloud. Files saved only on OneDrive will remain accessible online. Still, they won't take up space on your device's hard drive until you open them.

To turn on selective sync:
- Open the OneDrive app, click the **OneDrive icon in the taskbar,** and select **Settings**.
- Go to the **Account section** and click Choose **Folders**.
- Select or deselect the folders you want to sync locally. The deselected folders will remain in the cloud and be ready to download only when needed.

Microsoft 365 integration

OneDrive is seamlessly integrated with the **Microsoft 365** package, seamlessly making file management and collaboration seamless. You can save and open files directly from OneDrive within applications such as Word, Excel, PowerPoint, and Teams, making it easy to work on shared and synced documents. Real-time **co-authorship** allows you to work on documents simultaneously with other users, reducing wait times and improving productivity.

I use OneDrive for work and personal use, which is extremely useful for my productivity. OneDrive is Microsoft's cloud storage service that allows you to save, share, and sync your files quickly and securely. Thanks to OneDrive, I can access my documents from any device: smartphone, work PC, home computer, and tablet. This means I can start a project on my office computer, continue it on my tablet while on the go, and complete it at home on my PC without worrying about manually transferring files or losing the latest updated version.

Whenever I'm connected to the internet, all my files are automatically synced to every device. No matter what device I use, I can always be sure that I'm working on the latest version of the document without risking duplicates or confusion. This feature is handy for collaborating with colleagues, as they can easily share documents and set access permissions, allowing others to view or edit files in real time.

OneDrive also offers robust integration with other Office 365 applications like Word, Excel, and PowerPoint. I can open and edit files directly within these applications, automatically saving the changes to OneDrive. This built-in workflow helps me save time and reduce the chance of errors. For example, I'm working on a PowerPoint presentation. In that case, all the changes are saved in real time, and I can access them from my smartphone during a meeting to make a quick update.

Another handy feature of OneDrive is the ability to retrieve previous versions of a document. If I make a mistake or want to return to a prior file version, I can easily do so, thanks to the version history. This option gives me peace of mind, knowing that even if I make wrong changes, I can always return without losing important data.

Viewing and editing documents immediately is an advantage that helps me stay up-to-date and organized. I can access my files even when I don't have an internet connection, and all changes will be synced automatically when I'm back online. All these features make OneDrive an indispensable tool for improving my work and personal efficiency, allowing me to better manage my time and always be ready for any need.

11.   Microsoft 365 Copilot

Imagine having a personal assistant who is always available, discreet but powerful, and capable of helping you get the most out of every tool you use in your daily work. **Microsoft 365 Copilot** is a revolutionary AI integration designed to transform how you work and interact with the applications you already know and love. Copilot is not just a technological support but a valid extension of your skills, allowing you to face work challenges with greater simplicity, efficiency, and creativity.

Imagine typing a simple request and seeing professional documents, eye-catching presentations, or detailed analysis of complex data generated in seconds. This tool doesn't just execute commands; it understands context and adapts to your style, suggesting improvements and simplifying tasks that, until yesterday, would have taken hours. Its power doesn't stop at content creation: with Copilot, even the most everyday tasks, such as managing emails or preparing for a meeting, become remarkably intuitive. You can synthesize long conversations with just a few clicks, get personalized agendas, or retrieve critical information without frantically searching your files.

What makes Copilot unique is its ability to free you from repetitive tasks, giving you more time and mental space to focus on what matters: making strategic decisions, developing new ideas, and working with greater peace of mind. With continuous, personalized support, Copilot helps you stay in control, turning every workday into a chance to shine and achieve better results.

The promise of Microsoft 365 Copilot is ambitious but concrete: to create a work environment in which technological innovation is at the service of people, improving productivity and the quality of time we dedicate to work. It is a companion that grows with you, learns from your preferences, and allows you to tackle every task confidently, letting you finally focus on what you love to do most. This introduction will guide you to discover all the possibilities that Copilot offers, preparing you to make the most of its potential to revolutionize your approach to work.

Key features

Microsoft 365 Copilot is a breakthrough innovation designed to revolutionize how you work and interact with Microsoft 365 tools. With **automated content creation**, you can generate documents, presentations, and analytics quickly and accurately, saving time and improving the quality of results. Email **management** becomes intuitive, with the ability to synthesize long conversations and suggest effective responses, always keeping your inbox tidy.

Copilot also excels at **meeting support**, helping you prepare agendas, summarize previous discussions, and identify critical points for more productive interaction. On the data side, its **analysis and visualization capability** transforms complex numbers into clear charts and reports ready to be shared. Finally, the **integration with Microsoft 365 Chat** gives you instant access to information, allowing you to perform complex operations without interruption.

With Copilot by your side, every aspect of your daily work becomes more accessible, faster, and more personalized.

Automated Content Creation

One of the most revolutionary features of Microsoft 365 Copilot is its ability to automate content creation. Whether you need to draft a formal document, prepare a visually appealing presentation, or analyze large amounts of data, Copilot can assist you with accuracy and speed. A command is all it takes to generate detailed and well-structured drafts, summarize long reports, or improve already written texts with stylistic and grammatical suggestions. This functionality is not limited to mere automation: Copilot learns from your style and preferences, making each piece of content accurate and personalized.

Email management

Organizing your email has always been more complex and straightforward. With Microsoft 365 Copilot, you can manage long conversation threads without reading them entirely. The assistant summarizes messages in critical points, highlighting only what is relevant. In addition, it can suggest quick and contextualized answers, allowing you to save precious time and always keep your inbox under control. It is not only about speed but also about precision and the ability to grasp the meaning of the most complex communications.

Meeting Support

Microsoft 365 Copilot is an irreplaceable ally in meeting preparation and management. It can automatically generate agendas based on your goals, retrieve summaries of previous discussions, and even suggest relevant talking points. This means that every meeting can be approached with confidence and preparation. During meetings, Copilot can take notes in real-time, ensuring that no detail is missed and helping you conclude with a clear list of actions to take.

Data Analysis and Visualization

Working with data can be complex and time-consuming, but with Copilot, it becomes simple and intuitive. This tool allows you to create complex charts, reports, and visualizations with just a few commands, making even the most intricate datasets instantly understandable. Its ability to identify patterns and provide actionable insights makes it a valuable ally in making informed decisions. You don't need to be an expert in data analysis: Copilot turns numbers into stories, ready to be shared and presented.

Integration with Microsoft 365 Chat

One of Copilot's most significant innovations is its seamless integration with Microsoft 365 Chat, which ensures instant access to information and tools without ever leaving the application. This integration allows you to perform complex tasks in just a few steps, taking full advantage of the synergies between different Microsoft 365 applications. Whether you're working on a document, managing a project, or responding to an email, Copilot provides the support you need to streamline every workflow.

We are only at the beginning of an extraordinary transformation in the way you work and collaborate. **Microsoft 365 Copilot** is not just a practical help but a door wide open to the future of work, where artificial intelligence becomes your indispensable ally. Its current features are already revolutionary, but what makes this tool truly special is its growth potential. Copilot is set to evolve, integrating more and more into the applications you use daily and opening you up to new possibilities that we can only imagine today.

I invite you to stay updated on this evolution. Adopting and mastering technologies like this is an advantage and a real opportunity to transform how you approach your daily work. Keeping up with Copilot means being a protagonist of this revolution, ready to seize the opportunities that the future of work brings.

What you see today is just the beginning. Learning to fully utilize these tools will allow you to make a difference, transforming past practices into a more innovative, efficient, and future-oriented way of working. The future of work is already here, and you can be an active part of it. Take advantage of this opportunity!

12.   Advanced Tips and Tricks

This chapter will focus on **advanced tips and tricks** to optimize your workflow and save time, especially when using the **Microsoft 365** suite. As the applications and integrations available evolve, you can automate many repetitive tasks and improve your day-to-day project management. One essential tool for time optimization is **Power Automate**, which allows you to create automated workflows between different Microsoft 365 applications and beyond. This chapter will teach you the best techniques for **automating processes** and **syncing apps** to maximize productivity.

Advanced Tips to Optimize Time

Optimizing time is one of the main goals when working with the **Microsoft 365** suite. With advanced tools like **Power Automate**, you can automate many repetitive tasks that take up much of your day, significantly reducing downtime and improving overall efficiency. In this section, we'll explore how to use **Power Automate** to manage and automate these tasks, focusing on two key points: automating repetitive tasks and syncing between apps to improve productivity.

Automate repetitive tasks with Power Automate

Power Automate is one of the most potent tools for Microsoft users to create **automated workflows** that streamline their daily processes and tasks. This tool allows you to automate various operations without resorting to advanced programming. Here's how Power Automate can help you save time.

What is Power Automate, and how does it work?

Power Automate, formerly known as **Microsoft Flow**, is an application that allows you to create **automation between** different apps and services within the Microsoft ecosystem and with third-party apps. The basic concept is to create a workflow that, starting from a specific **trigger** (an action or event, such as receiving a new email), performs a series of predefined actions (such as archiving the email or sending a notification).

For example, you can configure Power Automate to:

- **Automatically save email attachments** to OneDrive or SharePoint when emails arrive from a specific contact.
- **Send notifications about Microsoft Teams** whenever a shared file is updated.
- **Automatically forward specific emails** to a co-worker or client without doing it manually.

Creating a workflow in Power Automate is intuitive, thanks to the user-friendly interface and pre-configured templates. Follow these steps to create a basic flow:

1. **Access Power Automate**: You can sign in directly from **Microsoft 365** or the dedicated Power Automate website.
2. **Select a flow template**: You can choose from hundreds of preset templates to automate everyday tasks, such as managing emails, archiving files, or creating reminders.

3. **Set the trigger**: The trigger is the event that starts the flow. For example, you can set a trigger when you receive an email from a specific customer, or when a new file is added to a shared folder on OneDrive.
4. **Configure actions**: Once you've defined the trigger, you can set the actions that will be performed automatically. For example, you can archive email, move files to a folder, or send notifications via Teams or Outlook.

Examples of common workflows

Here are some examples of workflows that can be created with Power Automate to optimize time:

- **Automatic email management**: You can set up a flow that automatically archives emails from a specific sender or keyword, reducing the time spent sorting through incoming mail.
- **Automated weekly reports**: With Power Automate, you can set up a flow that collects data from **Excel** or **SharePoint** and automatically generates a weekly report, which is then emailed to the intended recipients.
- **Task automation in Planner**: Power Automate can send an email or Teams notification to alert the task manager whenever a task is assigned on Microsoft Planner.

Benefits of using Power Automate

Key benefits of using Power Automate include:

- **Time savings**: You can focus on more complex and strategic tasks by automating repetitive tasks.
- **Error reduction**: Automating processes reduces the likelihood of human error.
- **Integration with other apps**: Power Automate seamlessly integrates with **Outlook**, **Teams**, **OneDrive**, **SharePoint**, **Excel**, and many other apps, allowing you to create workflows that connect multiple tools.

While there are several preset templates, you can customize each workflow to suit your specific needs by adding custom conditions and actions.

FAQ

1. **How do I access Microsoft Word, Excel, or PowerPoint online?** To access **Microsoft Word, Excel,** or **PowerPoint** online, visit the office.com site and sign in with your **Microsoft 365 account**. Here, you will find web versions of the applications, which you can use directly from the browser without installing any software on your device.

2. **What is the difference between OneDrive and SharePoint? OneDrive** is personal storage in the cloud, where you can keep and access your files from any device. **On** the other hand, SharePoint is a business collaboration platform allowing you to share files and collaborate on projects with teams and workgroups.

3. **How do I share a document in Word or Excel?** You can share a document directly from the application by clicking Share in the top right. From here, you can email a link or share the file directly with other users, allowing them to view or edit the Document.

4. **What are "macros" in Excel?** Macros in Excel are sequences of commands that automate repetitive tasks. They are handy for tasks that require the same steps repeatedly, such as processing data or generating reports.

5. **Can I use PowerPoint to create a presentation from scratch?** Absolutely yes! You can start with a **blank presentation** or choose one of the many **pre-made templates** offered by PowerPoint and customize slides, text, images, and animations.

6. **How can I work on a Word document with others in real time?** To collaborate on a Word document in real time, upload the File to **OneDrive** or **SharePoint** and share it with your colleagues. Multiple people can edit the Document simultaneously, and you'll see their changes in real time.

7. **How do I recover a previous version of a file in OneDrive?** OneDrive keeps a **version history of** your files. To retrieve an earlier version, right-click on the file and select **Version History**. From there, you can view and restore a prior file version.

8. **How can I customize the Ribbon in Excel?** To do so, click **File > Customize Ribbon**. From here, you can add, remove, or reorder commands to suit your personal preferences.

9. **Can I automate repetitive tasks in Access? Microsoft Access allows** you to use **macros** to automate repetitive tasks such as opening forms or running queries. You can create macros with an easy-to-use interface without programming in **VBA**.

10. **What are the advantages of using Microsoft Teams over email? Microsoft Teams** allows you to centralize conversations, file sharing, and project management, making communication smoother and more accessible than email. You can chat in real time, join virtual meetings, and work on shared documents simultaneously.

11. **How do I connect Microsoft Flow (Power Automate) to Excel to automate processes?** You can use **Power Automate to** link **Excel** to other apps or processes. For example, you can create a flow that sends a notification whenever a new record is added to an Excel sheet or automatically updates data in another document. Go to Power Automate, create a new flow, and select the Excel-related action to set your parameters.

12. **How can I integrate Outlook with OneNote to better manage my projects?** In **Outlook**, you can turn emails or appointments into **OneNote notes**. Just open the email or event and click **Send to OneNote**. From here, you can add details, organize information, and link notes to specific projects.

13. **Can I create complex workflows in SharePoint?** Yes, **SharePoint supports** creating **complex workflows** using **Power Automate**. You can set up document approval flows, automatic notifications, and project status updates, making managing teams and resources easier.

14. **How do I password-protect my files in Excel or Word?** To password-protect a file in Excel or Word, go to **file> File> Protect Document** and select **Encrypt with Password**. Enter your password and save the Document. Only those who know the password can access the file from that moment on.

15. **How do I sync data between Excel and Power BI for dynamic reporting?** Connect **Excel** to **Power BI** to generate real-time, dynamic, up-to-date reports. Import your data into Power BI and create visualizations based on Excel sheets. Every time you refresh your Excel sheet, the data in Power BI syncs automatically, allowing you to analyze information that's always up to date.

16. **How do I create a new document in Word online?** Go to office.com, sign in with your account, select **Word**, and click **New Blank Document**.

17. **How do I print a document in Excel?** To print a document in **Excel**, click **file> File** and select your desired printer. You can also configure the print area to choose which data to print.

18. **How do I recover a mistakenly deleted email in Outlook?** Go to the **Deleted Items folder** and look for the email you want to recover. Right-click and select **Move** to restore it to the desired folder.

19. **How do I add a contact to my address book in Outlook?** When you receive an email, you can right-click on the sender's name and select **Add to Contacts**. Fill in the details and save the contact.

20. **Can I use Office 365 applications on mobile devices?** You can download **the Word, Excel, PowerPoint, Outlook**, and **Teams apps** from the **App Store** or **Google Play** and sign in with your Microsoft 365 account.

21. **How do I share a calendar on Outlook?** Go to **Calendar** in Outlook, right-click on the calendar you want to share, and select **Share**. Please enter the email addresses of the people you want to share it with.

22. **Can I use the collaboration features on PowerPoint online?** Yes, in **PowerPoint Online**, you can collaborate with others in real-time. Share the link with your collaborators, and everyone can edit the presentation together.

23. **How do I insert a table in Word?** Click Insert > **Table** in Word and choose the number of rows and columns you want. You can then customize the table as you like.

24. **Can I add pictures to my notes in OneNote?** You can add photos to your notes in **OneNote** by clicking **Insert > Picture** and choosing an image from your device or OneDrive.

25. **How do I save a PowerPoint presentation to OneDrive?** When you save a presentation in **PowerPoint**, select **file> Files and choose OneDrive as** the location. Your presentation will be saved in the cloud and accessible from other devices.

26. **How do I organize my emails into folders on Outlook?** In **Outlook**, right-click on the **Folders section** and select **New Folder**. Name the folder and drag and drop the emails you want to organize.

27. **Can I collaborate on an Excel file with multiple people?** Yes, you can share an Excel file to **OneDrive** or **SharePoint and** work on it simultaneously with various people in real time.

28. **How do I add an eSignature in Outlook?** Go to **file> Files > Mail > Signatures**. Here, you can create a new signature, format it, and automatically add it to your emails.

29. **Can I password-protect my Excel files?** You can protect your Excel files with a password by going to **File > Info > Protect Workbook** and selecting **Encrypt with Password**.

30. **How do I change the Layout of a slide in PowerPoint?** Select the slide you want to change, click **Layout in** the Ribbon, and choose a new layout.

31. **How can I connect Power BI to Excel data to visualize it in real time?** You can connect Power BI to **Excel by** uploading the data to a **OneDrive** or **SharePoint** file. From Power BI, select the option to connect to an Excel file and choose the data you want to monitor in real time.

32. **How do I set up a certified digital signature on Word?** Go to **file> File> Protect Document> Add Digital Signature**. If you have a digital certificate installed, you can sign the Document electronically.

33. **How do I use Power Automate to synchronize data between SharePoint and Excel?** In **Power Automate**, create a new flow, choose **SharePoint** as the trigger (for example, when a new file is added), and set the action to automatically update an **Excel sheet** with the latest data.

34. **What is the best way to secure a shared Access database?** You can ensure a shared **Access database** using **SharePoint** or **OneDrive** permission levels. You can set specific permissions for each user, restricting access to certain data or tables.

35. **How do I use advanced queries in Access to extract complex data?** In **Access**, you can create **advanced queries** using SQL to extract specific data based on multiple criteria. For example, you can make a query that retrieves data from various tables and filters it to fields.

36. **Can I use Teams to schedule recurring meetings and invite external people?** You can schedule **recurring meetings** in Microsoft Teams by clicking **Calendar > New Meeting** and selecting the frequency. You can invite external people by entering their email addresses, even if they're not part of your organization.

37. **How do I use advanced find features in Outlook?** To find accurate emails, use the advanced search bar at the top and click Search **Tools > Advanced Find**. Then, enter specific criteria, such as keywords, senders, dates, etc.

38. **How do I use Excel's "Macro" function to automate calculations?** To use a **macro** in Excel, go to **View > Macro > Record Macro**. Do what you want to automate (like calculations or formatting) and stop recording. You can then repeat the macro to automatically perform the same set of operations.

39. **How do I manage file protection and sharing in Teams?** You can use the built-in OneDrive or SharePoint settings to do so. You can control who can view, edit, or share files, set access deadlines, and password-protect files.

40. **How do I create a link between Excel and Access to automate data import?** In **Access**, you can link to an Excel sheet using the **Link External Tables** feature. This lets you view and work on Excel data directly in Access, keeping it in sync in real-time.

41. **Can I use Excel to create a dynamic dashboard?** Yes, you can create a **dynamic dashboard** in Excel using pivot tables, charts, and advanced features like **Slicer** to update data in real time based on specific criteria.

42. **How can I use OneDrive to sync my files between multiple devices?** When you set up **OneDrive** on different devices, all files saved in synced folders are automatically updated on each device. Changes to one file on the file device will be replicated on all others.

43. **How do I set up an approval flow for documents on SharePoint?** Power Automate can set up a document approval flow in SharePoint. Whenever a document is uploaded or edited, it can be automatically sent to approvers for approval before it is finalized.

44. **How do I create an automatic index in Word?** You can create an **automatic table of contents using** heading styles. After you apply styles to headings, go to **References > Table of Contents** to generate an automatic table of contents based on your Document's headings and subheadings.

45. **How do I track resource usage in my projects on Microsoft Teams?** You can use **Microsoft Planner** or integrate tools like **Trello** into **Teams** to track resource allocation and task progress across projects, viewing everything directly within the Teams app.

Conclusion

We have reached the end of our journey through the nine main applications of Microsoft Office 365. I sincerely thank you for dedicating your time and attention to this guide. I hope you found the information presented helpful and easy to understand and apply daily.

Remember, this manual is designed to be by your side whenever needed. Whenever you use a particular application or wish to create a personalized workflow, you can refer to these pages for practical advice and immediate solutions. Technology is constantly evolving, and having a reliable resource can make all the difference in making your tasks more efficient and less stressful.

Throughout the book, I've shared numerous insights on utilizing artificial intelligence, both integrated within the Office suite and as a tool to significantly improve your productivity in your field of work and your personal life. AI represents a fascinating frontier that can transform your work, helping you perform complex tasks more simply and intuitively. This information has inspired you to explore new possibilities and integrate these technologies into your professional and personal journey.

Remember to download the **six exclusive bonuses** included with your purchase of this book. These additional resources have been specially created to deepen your skills further and offer practical tools to apply immediately. You'll find detailed guides, customizable templates, and other materials to help you take your abilities to the next level.

I wish you much happiness and serenity on your path. May the knowledge you've acquired open up new opportunities and make your work more efficient and rewarding. Success is not just a destination but a continuous journey of learning and growth. I'm delighted to have contributed in some way to your trip.

With warm regards, *Peter Patton*

Printed in Great Britain
by Amazon